New D...

Edited by **Sally Welch**   January–April 2021

The Bible Reading Fellowship
15 The Chambers, Vineyard
Abingdon OX14 3FE
brf.org.uk

The Bible Reading Fellowship (BRF) is a Registered Charity (233280)

ISBN 978 0 85746 970 0

This edition © The Bible Reading Fellowship 2020
Cover image © iStock.com/Ozbalci; illustration on page 139 © Martin Beek

Distributed in Australia by:
MediaCom Education Inc, PO Box 610, Unley, SA 5061
Tel: 1 800 811 311 | admin@mediacom.org.au

Distributed in New Zealand by:
Scripture Union Wholesale, PO Box 760, Wellington
Tel: 04 385 0421 | suwholesale@clear.net.nz

Acknowledgements
Scripture quotations marked NIV are taken from The Holy Bible, New International
Version, Anglicised edition, copyright © 1979, 1984, 2011 by Biblica. Used by
permission of Hodder & Stoughton Publishers, an Hachette UK company. All rights
reserved. 'NIV' is a registered trademark of Biblica. UK trademark number 1448790.

Scripture quotations marked NRSV are taken from The New Revised Standard
Version of the Bible, Anglicised Edition, copyright © 1989, 1995 by the Division of
Christian Education of the National Council of the Churches of Christ in the USA.
Used by permission. All rights reserved.

Scripture quotations marked NLT are taken from the Holy Bible, New Living
Translation, copyright © 1996, 2004, 2007, 2013. Used by permission of Tyndale
House Publishers, Inc., Carol Stream, Illinois 60188. All rights reserved.

Scripture quotations marked KJV are taken from the Authorised Version of the Bible
(The King James Bible), the rights in which are vested in the Crown, are reproduced
by permission of the Crown's Patentee, Cambridge University Press.

A catalogue record for this book is available from the British Library

Printed by Gutenberg Press, Tarxien, Malta

Suggestions for using *New Daylight*

Find a regular time and place, if possible, where you can read and pray undisturbed. Before you begin, take time to be still and perhaps use the BRF Prayer on page 6. Then read the Bible passage slowly (try reading it aloud if you find it over-familiar), followed by the comment. You can also use *New Daylight* for group study and discussion, if you prefer.

The prayer or point for reflection can be a starting point for your own meditation and prayer. Many people like to keep a journal to record their thoughts about a Bible passage and items for prayer. In *New Daylight* we also note the Sundays and some special festivals from the church calendar, to keep in step with the Christian year.

New Daylight and the Bible

New Daylight contributors use a range of Bible versions, and you will find a list of the versions used opposite. You are welcome to use your own preferred version alongside the passage printed in the notes. This can be particularly helpful if the Bible text has been abridged.

New Daylight affirms that the whole of the Bible is God's revelation to us, and we should read, reflect on and learn from every part of both Old and New Testaments. Usually the printed comment presents a straightforward 'thought for the day', but sometimes it may also raise questions rather than simply providing answers, as we wrestle with some of the more difficult passages of scripture.

New Daylight is also available in a deluxe edition (larger format). Visit your local Christian bookshop or BRF's online shop **brfonline.org.uk**. To obtain a cassette version for the visually impaired, contact Torch Trust for the Blind, Torch House, Torch Way, Northampton Road, Market Harborough LE16 9HL; +44 (0)1858 438260; **info@torchtrust.org**. For a Braille edition, contact St John's Guild, Sovereign House, 12–14 Warwick Street, Coventry CV5 6ET; +44 (0)24 7671 4241; **info@stjohnsguild.org**.

Comment on *New Daylight*

To send feedback, please email **enquiries@brf.org.uk**, phone **+44 (0)1865 319700** or write to the address shown opposite.

Writers in this issue

Amy Boucher Pye is a writer, speaker and retreat leader who runs the *Woman Alive* book club. She's the author of the award-winning *Finding Myself in Britain* (Authentic, 2015) and *The Living Cross* (BRF, 2016) and has an MA in Christian spirituality. Find her at **amyboucherpye.com**.

Terry Hinks is a United Reformed Church minister, serving two churches in the High Wycombe area. His particular concerns are for Christian unity, community engagement and the care of God's creation, alongside a long-standing love of stillness, biblical exploration and prayer.

Elizabeth Hoare is an ordained Anglican priest and teaches spiritual formation at Wycliffe Hall, Oxford. Her interests lie in the history and literature of Christian spirituality and their connections with today's world. She is married to Toddy, a priest and sculptor, and they have a teenage son.

Lakshmi Jeffreys is the rector (vicar) of a parish just outside Northampton. She combines this with being a wife, mother, friend, dog-walker, school governor and various other roles, within and beyond the wider church.

Ross Moughtin served in the same parish in Liverpool for 26 years, where with his wife Jacqui he led 50 Alpha courses. With four daughters, they have nine granddaughters and just one grandson. An international 800m runner in his prime, Ross is an enthusiastic member of his local ParkRun.

Margaret Silf is an ecumenical Christian committed to working across and beyond traditional divisions. She is the author of a number of books for 21st-century spiritual pilgrims and a retreat facilitator. She is a mother and grandmother and lives in north Staffordshire.

Naomi Starkey is a priest in the Church in Wales, based in a group of north Anglesey churches, and also works more widely as a pioneer evangelist.

Fiona Stratta works as a tutor and speech and drama teacher. She is author of *Walking with Gospel Women* (BRF, 2012) and *Walking with Biblical Women of Courage* (BRF, 2017). Throughout her writing, she desires to connect readers' spiritual journeys more closely to their daily lives.

Sheila Walker is an associate priest with three rural churches. She enjoys an eclectic mix of reading, writing, walking, assorted grandchildren and wasting time on puzzle pages.

Sally Welch writes…

I write this at the very beginning of a new year, looking at the illuminated decoration in the shape of a star which a clever carpenter has made and which sits now at the top of our church steeple. It is a visual reminder that 'the light shines in the darkness' and also that the 'darkness has not over-come it' (John 1:5, NIV). In the post-Christmas gloom that can sweep over us during the cold days of January, it is important to hold on to a belief in the light. This is particularly the case when we are facing death – our own or that of someone we love. Margaret Silf encourages us to take the brave step of exploring what death means to us, gently and generously leading us to the prayer that death is 'not the fracturing but the completion of the circle of life'.

On a more cheerful note, in her reflections on gladness and generosity (as part of BRF's Holy Habits initiative), Fiona Stratta invites us to participate in the 'virtuous circle: thanksgiving and praise give rise to gladness, which results in further praise, leading to more joy!' Elizabeth Hoare reminds us after Easter that 'no day can ever be ordinary, because Christ is risen', and we are encouraged by her to celebrate the risen Christ in every aspect of our lives, drawing us into the experience of self-giving love, which is at the heart of Christ and which is the aim of every follower of his.

In her reflections on the character of a saint, Amy Boucher Pye refers to her fortnight mid-Lent as being in the 'messy middle' of the season: 'We've passed the first rush of inspiration and the end isn't yet in sight.' We can feel that our faith journey has more than a touch of the 'messy middle' about it, which is why the new year can be a good time for bringing change into our prayer lives or Bible-reading patterns. Amy uses the list of Old Testament characters found in Hebrews 11 to remind us that 'messy' people too can be used by God and that all we need is to keep faith in the light.

I pray that the reflections you find in here will keep the light burning in your hearts and minds this season.

Sally Ann Welch

The BRF Prayer

Almighty God,
you have taught us that your word is a lamp for our feet
and a light for our path. Help us, and all who prayerfully
read your word, to deepen our fellowship with you
and with each other through your love.
And in so doing may we come to know you more fully,
love you more truly and follow more faithfully
in the steps of your Son Jesus Christ, who lives and reigns
with you and the Holy Spirit, one God forevermore.
Amen

Were you there? BRF celebrates its centenary in 2022 and we'd love you to share your BRF memories with us. We've already heard from supporters with wonderful stories. Beryl Fudge attended our 25th anniversary service in Westminster Central Hall in 1947, in the presence of the Queen Mother and Princess Margaret. Catharine Heron was prepared for confirmation in 1945 by our founder, Canon Leslie Mannering, and still has his duplicated notes in their original brown cardboard folder.

Do you have a BRF story to tell, whether of events, people, books or Bible reading notes? Please email **eley.mcainsh@brf.org.uk**, call **01865 319708** or write to **Eley McAinsh** at BRF, 15 The Chambers, Vineyard, Abingdon, OX14 3FE, United Kingdom.

Gladness and generosity

Gladness and generosity are holy habits* listed in the record of the believers' way of life in Acts 2:42–47. Jesus' followers are described as having glad and generous hearts. What a challenge! Are we glad enough? Are we generous enough? In any case, what is 'enough' and how do we measure such qualities as gladness and generosity? Perhaps our sense of inadequacy when considering this comes as a result of our view of God. Do we perceive God as a taskmaster, seeing if we are up to scratch? By contrast, knowing God as our loving Father, understanding all he has done for us and experiencing his ongoing grace lifts our hearts in trust that he will continue the work that he has begun in us (Philippians 1:6).

It is the Spirit's work within us that increasingly makes us into Christ's likeness. As we grow in the fruit of the Spirit, so we also grow in gladness and generosity. Developing holy habits is all about 'becoming' rather than about 'doing', although the doing helps us to become. Our hope and goal is that by looking at the world with the mind of Christ, ultimately the holy habits we cultivate will become instinctive. Growing in gladness and generosity is a journey that changes who we are, how we live and the choices we make.

What a wonderful new year's resolution – to determine to become increasingly glad and generous! As we start this new year, when resolutions are made and easily broken, may we realise that it is all about 'believing and receiving', not striving. We can only offer God our emptiness and weakness, and this humble act of trust in itself opens the door to new beginnings and an inpouring of the Spirit of God, who both gladdens our hearts and softens them to respond in generosity to others. Both striving and busyness war against our souls, whereas stillness and time with the Lord enable us to receive and grow in gladness and generosity. Let's make space this year for God and his work within us, so we grow in him and experience the joy and peace brought by glad and generous living.

FIONA STRATTA

*For more on BRF's Holy Habits programme, see **holyhabits.org.uk**. In the following reflections, quotations marked *GG* are from Andrew Roberts (ed.), *Holy Habits: Gladness and Generosity* (BRF, 2018).

A gift to appropriate

The spirit of the Lord God is upon me, because the Lord has anointed me; he has sent me… to comfort all who mourn; to provide for those who mourn in Zion – to give them a garland instead of ashes, the oil of gladness instead of mourning, the mantle of praise instead of a faint spirit. They will be called oaks of righteousness, the planting of the Lord, to display his glory.

We learn from these verses that gladness is first and foremost a gift: '*give* them' gladness instead of mourning and praise in place of a faint spirit. Any gift needs to be received, and action is often required to appropriate the gift. For example, receiving a piano is of little use unless we learn how to play it. God has blessed us with 'every spiritual blessing' (Ephesians 1:3), but, metaphorically speaking, *we* have to pour out the oil of gladness and put on and wear the mantle of praise. The Lord longs for us to thrive and has given us the means to do so, but we have to learn how!

Jesus quoted from this scripture when teaching in the Nazareth synagogue, saying these words were being fulfilled that very day, for 'the time of the Lord's favour' had come (Luke 4:19, NLT). He came promising life in all its fullness, and components of that full life are 'the oil of gladness' and 'the mantle of praise'.

Gladness and a praising spirit make us strong – we become 'oaks of righteousness'. Oak trees are hardy, mature, adaptable and resistant to disease; they do, however, consume a lot of water. This reminds us that to gain these qualities, we need to drink regularly from the spring of the water of life. As 'oaks of righteousness', we display the Lord's glory to those around us, for oaks are able to give shade in heat and shelter in rain. Like healthy oak trees that produce many acorns, we have the potential to bear much fruit.

Dear Lord, help us as we learn to rejoice always, pray without ceasing and be thankful in all circumstances (1 Thessalonians 5:16–18). As we do this, may we receive and appropriate your gift of gladness, becoming strong and fruitful, displaying your glory.

FIONA STRATTA

Counting our blessings

Always be full of joy in the Lord. I say it again – rejoice! Let everyone see that you are considerate in all you do… Don't worry about anything; instead, pray about everything. Tell God what you need, and thank him for all he has done… Fix your thoughts on what is true, and honourable, and right, and pure, and lovely, and admirable. Think about things that are excellent and worthy of praise.

We continue today thinking about appropriating the gift of gladness. In the fictional *Pollyanna* by Eleanor H. Porter, set in the early 20th century, the young orphan Pollyanna transforms the people in her community through the 'glad game', which she was taught by her missionary father. Whatever their circumstances, she encourages those she meets to find something to be glad about. Superficially this may seem like positive thinking, but the process of finding reasons to be glad profoundly alters the characters. Changing the way we think is transformative, growing in us humility, contentment and gladness. It takes a lifetime of learning!

The chorus of Johnson Oatman's 1897 hymn 'When upon life's billows' instructs: 'Count your blessings, name them one by one; count your blessings, see what God has done.' It is so easy to overlook God's daily provisions, yet gratitude is foundational to our relationship with God, changing our perspective. Becoming gratefully mindful opens our eyes to the delights around us.

Although we are told to 'fix' our thoughts and 'think about things that are excellent and worthy of praise' (v. 8), being called to rejoice 'full of joy in the Lord' (v. 4), we also recognise that we are not self-fixers. We are reliant on the Lord's presence to renew our joy and fill us with a deep, inner gladness, for 'gladness is more than just a happy or cheerful feeling' (*GG*, p. 7).

May we not be conformed to this world with its cynicism and despair, but be transformed by the renewing of our minds, experiencing gladness and joy. Then we can discern God's good, pleasing and perfect will for us, thriving as we live gladly and generously (see Romans 12:2).

'Unlock my heart. Free my spirit. Teach me to live as your child rather than as a beggar' (GG, p. 20).

FIONA STRATTA

Gladness in suffering

Because of our faith, Christ has brought us into this place of undeserved privilege where we now stand, and we confidently and joyfully look forward to sharing God's glory. We can rejoice, too, when we run into problems and trials, for we know that they help us develop endurance. And endurance develops strength of character, and character strengthens our confident hope of salvation. And this hope will not lead to disappointment. For we know how dearly God loves us, because he has given us the Holy Spirit to fill our hearts with his love.

As Pollyanna points out, God would not tell us to rejoice more than 800 times in the Bible unless he was serious about getting the message across! Choosing gladness makes us more appreciative, less anxious and more able to live 'a rich and satisfying life' (John 10:10). However, what can we be glad about when we are suffering and our hearts are breaking? As Christians we hold on to the realities and promises that give us strength, keeping our focus on God's generosity. We can be glad that beneath us are God the Father's everlasting arms. We can rejoice in Jesus, our Saviour, who promises a peace the world cannot give. We can be encouraged by the Holy Spirit, who fills our hearts with God's love, looking forward to the future joy of being with the Lord. In the hard times, we discover that gladness is an internal, intimate and objective joy that remains whatever the circumstances.

Meanwhile, during the storms of life, we can remain faithful in reading the Bible and in prayer, finding great consolation as God comforts us in our difficulties. Holding on to the promises of scripture strengthens and gladdens our hearts. Electing to praise and worship God in spite of our circumstances lifts our spirits. Fellowship and the caring concern of friends warm our aching hearts, cheering our souls. Like a candle flame, gladness shines most brightly in dark situations.

'All shall be well, and all shall be well and all manner of thing shall be well… He said not, "Thou shalt not be tempested, thou shalt not be travailed, thou shalt not be dis-eased"; but he said, "Thou shalt not be overcome"' (Julian of Norwich).

FIONA STRATTA

Trust and gladness

Trust in the Lord with all your heart; do not depend on your own understanding. Seek his will in all you do, and he will show you which path to take… I pray that God, the source of hope, will fill you completely with joy and peace because you trust in him. Then you will overflow with confident hope through the power of the Holy Spirit.

Our gladness and joy can be stolen by a loss or lack of trust. We are advised in these verses to have total trust in God rather than in our own abilities. It is as we fully trust in him that we experience peace and joy, making it possible for us to 'overflow with confident hope'. Gladness and anxiety do not go hand in hand, for as gladness grows through trust, anxiety decreases. For gladness and generosity to become rules of life in our personal discipleship, we need wholehearted trust in the shepherd's tender care and provision. We aspire to the simple trust of sheep who, knowing the love of the shepherd, follow with abandonment. Joyce Meyer summarises this transformative trust: believing God loves you; believing God is good; believing he has the power to help you; and believing he wants to help you.

Nurtured children live with a spontaneous joy and delight – they know how to be glad. Gradually life's blows and disappointments can threaten to erode this outlook. Childlike trust in God is the only remedy, and one that enables us to remain hope-filled and fruitful, even into old age. This hope in our hearts overflows as a gladness of disposition. As we trust ourselves to God's generosity, we can live generously for the interests of others, demonstrating the fruit of the Spirit: 'love, joy, peace, patience, kindness, goodness, faithfulness, gentleness, and self-control' (Galatians 5:22–23).

'This is the day, Lord, each day in your presence is a day of gladness and so we worship you, this day and always' (GG, p. 20). May it be a day in which we overflow with confident hope as we trust in you.

FIONA STRATTA

Overflow of gladness in worship and celebration

It is good to give thanks to the Lord, to sing praises to your name, O Most High; to declare your steadfast love in the morning, and your faithfulness by night, to the music of the lute and the harp, to the melody of the lyre. For you, O Lord, have made me glad by your work; at the works of your hands I sing for joy.

In these verses we are introduced to a virtuous circle: thanksgiving and praise give rise to gladness, which results in further praise, leading to more joy! Gladness makes us want to praise, and praising makes us glad. The best thing we can do when we experience a dearth of gladness is to praise God. This will invigorate our spirits and play a part in renewing and restoring us.

'It is good to give thanks to the Lord' (v. 1). It is good because thanksgiving brings glory to God. Praise is also good for us, for the joy of the Lord gives us strength (Nehemiah 8:10). As we worship, we are reminded of our purpose: 'to glorify God and to enjoy him forever' (Westminster Catechism).

We, like the psalmist, can consciously choose to develop a rhythm in our worship, focusing on God's love when waking and his faithfulness before sleeping. In addition, throughout the day, the sights, sounds and scents of creation, 'the works of your hands', draw us to further praise and gladness.

Music can play a huge part in our praise and worship, as can movement and dance. Joy is discovered and expressed as we worship with others. As Christian communities, we can party together as well as pray together. Celebration creates joy – Jesus performed his first gladness-giving miracle at a wedding party. 'Let's... celebrate each God-given day we have... experiment, take risks and have fun... Let's share our joy for life with those around us' (*GG*, p. 36).

But also, as Epiphany approaches, the magi, who in their joy bowed down and worshipped the Christ child, teach us that gladness can also be found in still and silent adoration.

Lord, 'confront me with your outrageous generosity, your wasteful, extravagant love, your wild freedom, your exuberant joy!' (GG, p. 20).

FIONA STRATTA

Overflow of gladness into generosity

Remember this: whoever sows sparingly will also reap sparingly, and whoever sows generously will also reap generously. Each of you should give what you have decided in your heart to give, not reluctantly or under compulsion, for God loves a cheerful giver. And God is able to bless you abundantly, so that in all things at all times, having all that you need, you will abound in every good work… You will be enriched in every way so that you can be generous on every occasion, and through us your generosity will result in thanksgiving to God.

It is essential to become well grounded in our understanding that it is God's will for us to rejoice and experience gladness. As gladness takes root in our hearts and personalities, we incline more naturally to generosity of heart towards others. The natural overflow of this will be acts of generosity, sharing our finances, possessions, resources, hospitality, time and talents. Generosity is primarily a response to God's grace and extravagant love for us. Our resulting gratitude and thanksgiving give rise not only to worship but also to mission.

Today's passage suggests that we need organisation and discipline in our giving, but this is not at odds with glad generosity. We are to behave generously not only when the mood takes us, although there will be times for spontaneous, emotionally triggered giving. We also need to remember that, at different points in our lives, there will be 'seasons' for giving and receiving. It takes grace to receive gladly as well as to give, accepting others' generosity with gratitude. Even when we are limited in our ability to give to others (for example, by financial or health issues), we can remain generous-hearted towards God in worship and prayer.

A Spirit-empowered life enables us to give from a spring of fullness that he replenishes, rather than from a duty-bound cistern that can dry up. When we give of ourselves, we will need renewal, following our Lord's example of taking time with the Father.

Lord, we know that it is not what we have but what we do with it that matters, recognising that 'all things come from you, and of your own have we given you' (1 Chronicles 29:14, NRSV).

FIONA STRATTA

Generosity of being

There were two blind men sitting by the roadside. When they heard that Jesus was passing by, they shouted, 'Lord, have mercy on us, Son of David!' The crowd sternly ordered them to be quiet; but they shouted even more loudly, 'Have mercy on us, Lord, Son of David!' Jesus stood still and called them, saying, 'What do you want me to do for you?' They said to him, 'Lord, let our eyes be opened.' Moved with compassion, Jesus touched their eyes. Immediately they regained their sight and followed him.

When we think of generosity, we may automatically think of giving financially and materially, and indeed this is one aspect of a generous lifestyle. Open-handed giving is found throughout the Bible to be part of God-fearing and God-glorifying living. But Jesus was not affluent, and his generosity was of a different nature. As we see in today's verses, Jesus' ministry was encapsulated by generosity of time (he halts his journey for these men), of body (he touches their eyes, affirming them as he heals them) and of soul and spirit (he is moved with compassion, open to all, whatever their social status). Jesus has a generosity of being that results in a generosity of doing. His motivation for generosity is pure, stemming from compassionate love.

The question Jesus asks the blind men is both simple and profound: 'What do you want me to do for you?' At first glance the answer seems obvious, yet this question shows that generosity is not to be forced on people; rather it is sensitive, aware of the uniqueness of the individual. Generosity seeks to understand before it draws conclusions and contributes. It holds back from making critical judgements (unlike the crowd in this scene), aiming instead for legitimate discernment. It requires wisdom.

To maintain this generosity of being, we seek the daily infilling of the Holy Spirit (Ephesians 5:18). We must beware of giving to such an extent that the living water within us becomes a mere trickle. In silence we can reflect, pray, replenish and learn wisdom.

'The more we receive in silent prayer, the more we can give in our active life. We need silence to be able to touch souls' (Mother Teresa of Calcutta).

FIONA STRATTA

Generous living

In his grace, God has given us different gifts for doing certain things well. So if God has given you the ability to prophesy, speak out with as much faith as God has given you. If your gift is serving others, serve them well. If you are a teacher, teach well. If your gift is to encourage others, be encouraging. If it is giving, give generously. If God has given you leadership ability, take the responsibility seriously. And if you have a gift for showing kindness to others, do it gladly.

These verses tear down the artificial barriers that we tend to create between spiritual gifting and human gifting, for all is God-given. Being practical and being spiritual go hand in hand. Whatever our talents and whatever we do, giving of ourselves with glad, wholehearted commitment is the substance of generous living. We benefit, too, in that we receive threefold when showing kindness to others: positive hormones are released as we plan or contemplate carrying out an act of kindness, then again as we carry it out and finally once more as we remember the act.

Generously giving of oneself, however, is not confined to acts of service and contribution of talents. Another aspect of generous living, seen so clearly in the life of Jesus, is that of enabling others to develop their identity, gifts and potential. Generous living embraces generous attitudes – 'be encouraging' (v. 8); 'bear with each other and forgive one another' (Colossians 3:13, NIV). From these heart attitudes come our words. Let us be quick to speak generous, affirming words and slow to find fault. It takes generosity and courage to speak of our life experiences, especially the painful ones, in order to help and bless others. Yet disclosing our weaknesses or failings may free others to reveal their vulnerabilities. We can become generous listeners, rich in tolerance, compassion and understanding, enabling people to feel accepted and valued.

'Most gracious God, all good things come from you and are signs of your love. May our gratitude fill us with gladness, and our gladness with generosity, that we may express our joy in the service of others, and give in thankfulness for what we have received, through Jesus Christ our Lord. Amen' (GG, p. 14).

FIONA STRATTA

A joyous challenge

'Do to others as you would have them do to you… Be merciful, just as your Father is merciful. Do not judge, and you will not be judged; do not condemn, and you will not be condemned. Forgive, and you will be forgiven; give, and it will be given to you. A good measure, pressed down, shaken together, running over, will be put into your lap; for the measure you give will be the measure you get back.'

These verses summarise what we have been considering – a generosity that embraces our whole lifestyle. As we give of ourselves through God's grace, we experience the satisfaction of knowing that we have made a difference in the lives of others. Whether large or small, this gladdens our hearts, and the overflow of our rejoicing leads to further acts of generosity.

There is, however, a challenge for the Christian whose heart is set on growing in the holy habit of gladness and generosity. We are taught by Jesus in these verses that when we are generous, we will receive abundantly. Yet we do not give with the goal of receiving, which would be manipulative and hypocritical. Nevertheless, we know we will receive, for this is promised in these verses. The challenge is to have sincere hearts as we live generously. This sincerity was apparent in the believers as they met together (Acts 2:46) – in fact 'generous hearts' (NRSV) is sometimes translated as 'sincere hearts' (NIV). Paul wrote to Timothy saying that love should come from 'a pure heart, a good conscience, and sincere faith' (1 Timothy 1:5).

We do not necessarily receive like for like in return for our generosity, but there will be 'a good measure, pressed down, shaken together, running over' (v. 38). We may receive unexpected blessings, such as friendship, contentment, identity, a sense of purpose and fulfilment. Ultimately, for the Christian, our goal in generous living is to bring glory to God: 'Let your light shine before others, that they may see your good deeds and glorify your Father in heaven' (Matthew 5:16, NIV).

Lord, may we be 'overwhelmed by your extravagance, transformed
by your generosity and liberated by your abundance to be
the answer to the prayers of others. Amen' (GG, p. 22).

FIONA STRATTA

Psalms 29—42

 We've been made with a facility to share our lives with God: for relationship with him. And whatever we may be going through, however we may be feeling, we are designed to share all this with our loving creator. He knows us through and through; there is no point in pretence.

So at the very heart of the Bible we find the book of Psalms, a collection of songs offered to God from the people of Israel, chosen to bring his wonderful blessings to a broken world. The very name of this book, Psalms, is derived from the Greek word for instrumental music. In fact, many psalms are introduced with a musical reference.

Singing engages the whole of our personality, whatever we may be thinking and however we may be feeling. How often do we find ourselves singing a hymn or chorus when we feel either particularly blessed or the very opposite, during a time of great need? The psalms encourage us to sing to God.

At some stage in Israel's history, probably after the return from exile in faraway Babylon, some 150 psalms were brought together as a hymn book for the restored temple of Jerusalem. Here they were sung together, a shared experience in worshipping God and now a shared experience over the generations. These psalms are admittedly very old and derived from a culture very different from our own. Even so, across the millennia, they come to us as surprisingly relevant. We can see ourselves in the struggles; we have the same questions about life, the same anxieties, the same hopes.

From childhood Jesus would have known these songs, as we know our favourite hymns. He would have sung them with his disciples, such as during their last meal together. As we will discover he drew on their resource during a time of terrible testing.

For the next two weeks we are going to be making some of these psalms our own. They come from a whole variety of situations, often from times of stress, even of despair, but they are always open and intensely honest. Above all, they encourage us to orientate our lives towards God, assured of his attention and confident of his response.

ROSS MOUGHTIN

We serve a great God

The voice of the Lord shakes the desert; the Lord shakes the Desert of Kadesh. The voice of the Lord twists the oaks and strips the forests bare. And in his temple all cry, 'Glory!' The Lord sits enthroned over the flood; the Lord is enthroned as King forever. The Lord gives strength to his people; the Lord blesses his people with peace.

When God speaks he speaks with power, his voice as thunder shakes even the solid earth. His authority resists all challenges, effortlessly. And here is our security.

One saying which has sustained me in ministry over the years is from Hudson Taylor: 'You do not need a great faith, but faith in a great God.' For the wonder is that this God of awesome majesty chooses to bless his people; we focus on him in his power rather than on ourselves in our frailty.

The reference to the Desert of Kadesh would have touched a raw nerve for the people of Israel. This is the very place where they failed to enter their promised land, intimidated by the reports from the spies sent in advance by Moses to reconnoitre the land. It was a prosperous land, yes – but peopled by powerful inhabitants. They drew back simply because they failed to reckon on God's authority to give them victory. They listened to their fears and not to God. Even so, God persevered with his people, and under the leadership of one of those spies, Joshua, they were to claim their promised land. Their weakness was no problem to God: the Lord gives strength to all who acknowledge his kingship.

For we serve a God who is enthroned over the flood, over everything that would overwhelm or subdue us. Whatever our situation today, we need to affirm this by praising God in his glory and breathtaking power.

The key is to focus on him and not on ourselves, to understand that whatever would menace us, God's power is greater, much greater. There's simply no contest. He gives strength to his people, and so we refuse to be intimidated by anyone who would challenge him. And his glorious rule brings shalom, an all-embracing peace which encompasses his entire creation.

Let us join with everyone in his temple and cry, 'Glory!'

ROSS MOUGHTIN

Keep on relying

I will exalt you, Lord, for you lifted me out of the depths and did not let my enemies gloat over me. Lord my God, I called to you for help, and you healed me. You, Lord, brought me up from the realm of the dead; you spared me from going down to the pit. Sing the praises of the Lord, you his faithful people; praise his holy name.

We are at our most vulnerable when we become complacent, when we think we can rely on our own strength and ability. Life seems good; we're doing okay. We even presume on God, simply taking him and his care for granted. This is what happened to the writer of this psalm. Looking back on their experience, they tell us: 'When I felt secure, I said, "I shall never be shaken"' (v. 6).

Then something happened. For them, it seems to have been a life-threatening illness, but it could be any kind of crisis. One moment everything seems fine; next moment, the very ground beneath our feet gives way. We hit rock bottom to despair of life itself. Devoid of hope, the future seems bleak indeed. Our cries for help go seemingly unheard. People mock us; even God, it seems, in his anger hides his face from us.

Except that he doesn't. As water is drawn from a deep well, so God raises us up from the deepest pit. When we can see no way out of the darkness, remarkably he comes to our aid. Now overwhelmed with his grace, we rejoice in our rescue. So we invite all God's people to join us in a dance of praise, to celebrate the God of our salvation. No longer the drab sackcloth of mourning, we want to share our experience of God's incredible mercy. 'We had it coming to us – but even so, God came to our help!'

Here in this psalm we have life written large, from proud self-reliance through deep despair to exuberant celebration. The challenge is to live our lives, even our ordinary everyday lives, with a resolve to keep relying on God's grace and a resolution, however we may be feeling, to praise him for his goodness.

Join in with the psalmist: 'Lord my God, I will praise you forever' (v. 12).

ROSS MOUGHTIN

Take hold of hope

In you, Lord, I have taken refuge; let me never be put to shame; deliver me in your righteousness. Turn your ear to me, come quickly to my rescue; be my rock of refuge, a strong fortress to save me. Since you are my rock and my fortress, for the sake of your name lead and guide me. Keep me free from the trap that is set for me, for you are my refuge. Into your hands I commit my spirit; deliver me, Lord, my faithful God.

Psalms are there to be used, to be sung or said, together or by ourselves. We can take their words and make them our own. They connect us with God's faithful people throughout the generations; they give context to our experiences.

As an observant Jew, Jesus would have known this psalm as part of his evening prayers, committing himself to his Father's care each night before falling asleep. So, as he hangs on the cross, his final words are a loud cry: 'Father, into your hands I commit my spirit' (Luke 23:46). Here Jesus not only shouts out this one verse but takes hold of this whole psalm to speak of his trust in his Father's deliverance in a situation totally devoid of hope. He holds on to the experience of God's people throughout the generations.

This psalm begins with a decision, a resolve to make the Lord our refuge on the basis that he promises to protect his people. Often this trust may appear foolish, and we risk ridicule. I can recall being savaged in the local press for our church's building project, which seemed to have completely failed. What hurt most was being mocked for our trust in God's guidance and the implication that he had let us down. So, when the ministry centre opened, it was God's name that was vindicated. Wonderfully, to a watching world, he proved himself faithful in an amazing way.

Certainly, this is the experience of this psalm, of encountering hostility from those who would catch us out in our determination to live for God.

---

*A message for us today? 'Be strong and take heart,
all you who hope in the Lord' (v. 24).*

ROSS MOUGHTIN

Holding nothing back

For day and night your hand was heavy on me; my strength was sapped as in the heat of summer. Then I acknowledged my sin to you and did not cover up my iniquity. I said, 'I will confess my transgressions to the Lord.' And you forgave the guilt of my sin. Therefore let all the faithful pray to you while you may be found; surely the rising of the mighty waters will not reach them. You are my hiding-place; you will protect me from trouble and surround me with songs of deliverance.

It's strange how sometimes we do our best to avoid God. We resent his claim on our lives; we refuse to let go of something which we know dishonours him. We decide to go it alone.

Except that we can't. We know in our bones that we can't live our lives without him. Evading God is draining; it saps our energy, as we deny ourselves the joys of his unfailing love. Try as we can, we know we can't keep blocking him out. Sooner or later we will have to give in and give up what we know to be wrong. It might as well be sooner rather than later! It's not easy, but we decide to own up to our disobedience. So, we take a deep breath and return to God: we say sorry for keeping our distance. We admit our avoidance and confess our transgression.

Wonderfully, yet once again, God receives us with joy as he freely forgives us. There is a sense of both relief and restoration. We're back with God, our refuge; once more we may delight in his blessings. Now, rather than hiding from God, we find in him our hiding place, our security in an insecure world. Troubles will not overwhelm us. He guides our path. No longer are we knocked about by life, pushed around by events. Instead we may rely on his guidance. We may hear his voice directing our path and preparing our way. Wherever we go, we can count on his unfailing love. Such knowledge makes all the difference.

Ask yourself the question: am I holding anything back from God?

ROSS MOUGHTIN

Our help and our shield

No king is saved by the size of his army; no warrior escapes by his great strength. A horse is a vain hope for deliverance; despite all its great strength it cannot save. But the eyes of the Lord are on those who fear him, on those whose hope is in his unfailing love, to deliver them from death and keep them alive in famine. We wait in hope for the Lord; he is our help and our shield.

In an insecure world, where are we to find our security? This has to be the key question as we live our lives. We may choose to rely on our abilities, however modest we may strive to appear. Or count on our assets, financial or otherwise, as an investment to see us through. We may choose to bank on our friendships or family. Whatever it may be, the ongoing temptation is to rely on our own resources in the same way a ruler would rely on the might of their military. Whatever the threat, they know their army will keep them safe. Just look at my magnificent warhorses!

The reality is that we are so easily impressed by displays of human power, especially our own – until they are found wanting. The wonder is that God, who spoke this incredible universe into existence, invites us to entrust our lives to him. His passion for justice means he is active in our world, continually thwarting the purposes of those who would plan evil, even against us. This is something to celebrate. So this psalm opens with a fanfare of praise as we rejoice in God's unfailing love. We are called to worship him with music, praise which engages the whole of our personality, even with a ten-stringed lyre (or its modern equivalent).

But in this world, we are not there yet. Death still intimidates; famine is still to be banished. Nevertheless, we know that God will keep his word whatever the cost and so we may wait in hope, confident of his faithfulness. With great joy this psalm encourages us to hold on, to make our God our security.

'May your unfailing love be with us, Lord,
even as we put our hope in you' (v. 22).

ROSS MOUGHTIN

Praise God whatever

I will extol the Lord at all times; his praise will always be on my lips. I will glory in the Lord; let the afflicted hear and rejoice. Glorify the Lord with me: let us exalt his name together. I sought the Lord, and he answered me; he delivered me from all my fears. Those who look to him are radiant; their faces are never covered with shame.

Our worship of God is at its most powerful when we decide to praise him whatever our situation, however we may be feeling. We may feel discouraged or daunted; we may be experiencing loss or loneliness. Whatever the case, this psalm begins with a resolve to praise God, come what may.

We fly by instruments, not always able to see the landscape below us, trusting in its existence. And we are called to articulate our praise, out loud with our lips. We are to sing or speak our worship as a deliberate decision; we refuse to be cowed. We keep at it regardless. Such praise honours God for his unfailing love, as we extol him for his unchanging faithfulness. Wonderfully, he is our refuge at all times and in every situation. Above all, such praise is to be shared, so this psalm invites others to participate. We call on others to join with us in our song of thanksgiving, even and especially those going through tough times. We encourage them to sing with us and to leave their difficulties with God.

To demonstrate that we are to praise God in every situation, this psalm is acrostic; that is, each verse begins with successive letters of the Hebrew alphabet – it's the A to Z of worship. It will have made composing the psalm more challenging but will have made it easier to remember, which may well be important if you are in pain or in panic.

Such praise is transformative; it changes us. Our situation may not change, but our perspective certainly will as we focus on God and his promises. No longer in the grip of anxiety, even our appearance may change. Such people simply glow in the dark. What is stopping you now from joining with the psalmist and speaking or singing out the praise of the Lord?

'Taste and see that the Lord is good;
blessed is the one who takes refuge in him' (v. 8)

ROSS MOUGHTIN

Under attack

Contend, Lord, with those who contend with me; fight against those who fight against me. Take up shield and armour; arise and come to my aid. Brandish spear and javelin against those who pursue me. Say to me, 'I am your salvation.' May those who seek my life be disgraced and put to shame; may those who plot my ruin be turned back in dismay.

'An unholy row has erupted following claims that a local vicar has divided his parish.' Our local newspaper laid into me in a big way because of our plan to build a £1.3 million ministry centre, which was opposed by some members of the community. But this is what happens when we seek to advance God's cause – we take flak; we experience opposition which can seem more than simply a human pushback.

The big question is: how should we respond? We can always fight back – but that can be both draining and dangerous. In the case of our church community, we decided to work so that when the centre finally opened, such was its success that those who 'plotted against us' ended up apologising for their opposition.

This is the kind of experience behind this psalm. As God's servant, the writer was being attacked by powerful people. However, their real goal was God himself; they were just using the writer to get at God. In such cases, we must remember that the battle is therefore God's and not ours. And this insight makes all the difference as we look to him as our defender. The reality is that we can trust God to protect and provide for those who seek to serve him. So the psalmist may confidently call on God to act in power as he comes to their rescue. Above all, the request is for a vindication of that trust.

However, when we pray in the spirit of this psalm, we need to be completely honest with God – and with ourselves. Is this God's cause or just ours, merely the outcome of our own selfish ambition?

Heavenly Father, help me to put my trust in you to defend and protect me.

ROSS MOUGHTIN

To delight in God's love

How priceless is your unfailing love, O God! People take refuge in the shadow of your wings. They feast in the abundance of your house; you give them drink from your river of delights. For with you is the fountain of life; in your light we see light. Continue your love to those who know you, your righteousness to the upright in heart. May the foot of the proud not come against me, nor the hand of the wicked drive me away.

We worship a great God, who delights in blessing his people, even with extravagance. His gift of life richly overflows; his wonderful creation is aglow with his light. Our privilege is to enjoy his care and to rely on his faithfulness.

So why is God so readily rejected by so many people? Why is it that they live their lives without him, even against him? We live in a world where our wonderful God is not only derided but dismissed by people caught up in their own vanity. They plot evil and speak lies against us. This is where this psalm begins: how can people be so wicked? What makes them kick us around, push us aside? How it is that such people so freely disregard God's passion for justice?

The fundamental reason is simple, as shown in the opening verse: 'There is no fear of God before their eyes.' Such people refuse to honour God: they are determined to deny him any claim on their lives. But surely this 'fear of God' does not mean that we should be frightened of him while also delighting in him. God is not capricious, kind one moment and threatening the next. The answer – as seen in this psalm – is to focus on the scale of God's steadfast love. As we appreciate the full extent of his faithfulness, so we naturally want to live for him, celebrating the wonder of his grace.

The first step of living for God is simple – to realise how much we are loved, against every expectation. 'Love so amazing, so divine, demands my soul, my life, my all' ('When I survey the wondrous cross', Isaac Watts, 1707).

Take a moment to delight in God's incredible love.

ROSS MOUGHTIN

Decide to trust

Do not fret because of those who are evil or be envious of those who do wrong; for like the grass they will soon wither, like green plants they will soon die away. Trust in the Lord and do good; dwell in the land and enjoy safe pasture. Take delight in the Lord, and he will give you the desires of your heart.

To live for God is to enjoy his rich blessings. So how is it that those who turn their backs on him seem to be better off than us? We see rich people taking advantage of the weak and vulnerable. Not only do they get away with it, but they even seem to prosper. Life does not seem to be fair.

As a result, we face the ongoing temptation of being impressed by the lifestyle of the rich and powerful; we may even seek to imitate them. Worse still, we face the danger of thinking that God appears to be indifferent to how we live: why bother serving God when those who don't serve him appear to flourish? There seems to be no incentive in seeking his will for our lives.

But, as the psalmist would teach us, this is a foolish and short-sighted conclusion. We need to step back and see the big picture, to realise what happens to those who have no time for God. Their wealth is transient; their happiness is fleeting. Here we have another acrostic psalm: it's an A-to-Z guide on how to live your life, very much part of the wisdom tradition. If you are going to enjoy life, there are some key principles to follow. Above all, we need the resolve to make God our guide and teacher, and more – to delight in him.

It's not going to be easy. Sometimes we just have to pause and reflect, refusing to be taken in by the false promises of an easy prosperity. We need resilience against life's shocks and disappointments. Come what may, we are going to entrust our lives to God, to embrace his cause, whatever the short-term costs.

This day, 'commit your way to the Lord;
trust in him and he will do this' (v. 5).

ROSS MOUGHTIN

Holding nothing back

Lord, do not rebuke me in your anger or discipline me in your wrath. Your arrows have pierced me, and your hand has come down on me. Because of your wrath there is no health in my body; there is no soundness in my bones because of my sin. My guilt has overwhelmed me like a burden too heavy to bear.

'Lord, help me. I'm about to fall!' How often do we cry out to God for help? This psalm shows us how.

First, it is realistic. Clearly the psalmist is in some distress, using image after image to convey some terrible suffering. Their wounds are open and fester; they are in severe pain. Their heart races; they are unable even to speak, let alone hear. It seems that everyone is out to get them and is gloating over their misery. More than all this, even their close friends give them a wide berth, finding the psalmist's injuries abhorrent. No detail is spared. They have hit rock bottom, with no way out. Sharing our predicament with God – telling him how it is and holding nothing back – is at the heart of true prayer. No stiff upper lip here.

But more than this, the psalmist is prepared to see God himself at work. When it comes down to the basics, it is God's anger. There is no sidestepping the issue here: God himself is firing the arrows. But why? Here the psalmist admits the truth about themselves: it's their guilt. If they are suffering, it is simply the result of their own wilful disobedience. God has every right to be angry with them for what they have done.

At the very heart of this psalm is the conviction that God can take it. Such is his compassion that there is no need to hide behind some false piety. To share our lives with God means sharing our deepest thoughts with him. Even if they frighten us, they don't faze him. He doesn't shut us down or tell us to be quiet. And so we cry out to God in our need. He alone is our refuge; he alone promises to hear our cries for help.

Do we find being honest with God difficult?

ROSS MOUGHTIN

Our only hope

You have made my days a mere handbreadth; the span of my years is as nothing before you. Everyone is but a breath, even those who seem secure. Surely everyone goes around like a mere phantom; in vain they rush about, heaping up wealth without knowing whose it will finally be. But now, Lord, what do I look for? My hope is in you.

There are times when we become only too aware of our own mortality. Conducting funeral services for those who are younger than me, who have died of 'natural causes', makes me pause and reflect on my own transience. We know only too well that our days are numbered, just a fleeting passage of time. This is how the psalmist shares their innermost thoughts with God. All human striving is, to say the least, time-limited. However much wealth we may hope to accumulate, at the end of the day, and more to the point at the end of our lives, it is worthless.

Such thinking, of course, is profoundly unsettling, and we do our best to push such thoughts to the back of our minds and get on with life. It's not the kind of thing people want to hear. But the psalmist persists, refusing to keep quiet. Something has happened – an illness, a disappointment. It makes us realise that we have no security in this life, nothing to hold on to. We ask God how much longer we have left.

However, the fact that we can share our deepest fears with God means everything. We may feel utterly insignificant, but the reality is the very opposite: we can address God, knowing that he will not just listen but even respond. He, and he alone, gives us value; his attention gives us significance. What our trials show only too clearly is that our only hope is in God himself. Nowhere else will we find permanence, a future.

We may not understand what is happening to us, but we do understand that we can go to God for help. And this makes all the difference.

However you may be feeling today, simply say to God, 'My hope is in you.'

ROSS MOUGHTIN

Keep on waiting

I waited patiently for the Lord; he turned to me and heard my cry. He lifted me out of the slimy pit, out of the mud and mire; he set my feet on a rock and gave me a firm place to stand. He put a new song in my mouth, a hymn of praise to our God. Many will see and fear the Lord and put their trust in him.

I hate waiting. Whether it is standing in a supermarket queue or waiting for a friend to arrive, it is clearly a waste of my valuable time and also cedes control to others as they keep me waiting. I get restless. Yet waiting is part and parcel of living for God, resting in his purposes and relying on his timing. For his timescale is different to ours. How often does he tell us to be patient and wait?

This psalm is about how to wait for God, and significantly it comes from a time of considerable stress. You would not realise this in the way the psalm begins, but the psalmist says that 'troubles without number surround me' (v. 12). People are out to get them; they even desire the psalmist's ruin (v. 14). In all this the psalmist is totally honest – much of this is their fault, the result of their own disobedience: 'My sins have overtaken me, and I cannot see' (v. 12). All this means that they cannot find a way out.

What do we do in the same situation? We can reflect on those times when we found God to be faithful. This psalm opens with an experience of God's faithfulness, how he rescued the writer from a similarly hopeless situation. We too can recall when we had lost our footing and were in danger of going under. We can relive how we had to wait for God to respond. When he did, we remember how we wanted to burst into a song of praise and to share our experience with others. Our trust in God was vindicated then, so we know we will find him faithful yet again. As ever, we rely on his resources and not our own. So the psalm ends: 'You are my help and my deliverer; you are my God, do not delay' (v. 17).

Where are you waiting for God?

ROSS MOUGHTIN

Confidence in God

Even my close friend, someone I trusted, one who shared my bread, has turned against me. But may you have mercy on me, Lord; raise me up, that I may repay them. I know that you are pleased with me, for my enemy does not triumph over me. Because of my integrity you uphold me and set me in your presence forever.

We've all been wounded by a friend, someone we thought we could trust but who to our dismay turned against us. There's a deep hurt in being let down, a sense of betrayal. This is the experience underlying this psalm, composed during a time of weakness, probably a life-threatening illness. The future looks grim, and the psalmist needs the support of friends, indeed of anyone who could bring some encouragement, even a glimmer of hope. However, it seems that everyone has turned against him, even willing his very worst: 'A vile disease has afflicted him; he will never get up from the place where he lies' (v. 8). Hardly the words we would want to hear. Even his closest friends, when they were most needed, have instead deserted him.

This is the psalmist's perception of what is happening during his time of tough testing. Whether or not this is actually the case is beside the point: this is how he feels – abandoned, utterly alone. However, the psalmist can share all this with God. He may have lost the trust of his friends, but even in the darkest of times he is assured of God's presence, confident of his care and reliant on his resources, come what may.

Such is God's mercy that there is no way he will ever abandon us, even if we have brought all this on ourselves. This understanding alone gives the confidence to hope, even to trust. The healing we seek from the Lord includes not just our physical condition but, just as important, our relationships too.

At the very basic level, this is all we need – to know the complete faithfulness of the Lord. So we do not fear the future, come what may.

Share any experience of being badly let down with the God who will never fail us.

ROSS MOUGHTIN

Our thirst assuaged

As the deer pants for streams of water, so my soul pants for you, my God. My soul thirsts for God, for the living God. When can I go and meet with God? My tears have been my food day and night, while people say to me all day long, 'Where is your God?'

Walking the Cumbria Way in hot weather meant we soon used up our water. So when we eventually reached a pub, it was sheer bliss to drink a pint of lemonade – and then another one. We've all experienced such a moment, a desperate thirst being wonderfully assuaged. And this is how the psalmist shares their experience during a time of great longing for God, looking to him alone for complete fulfilment.

But why the deer? This psalm comes from the heights of Hermon (v. 6) to the north of Israel, where melting snow contributes to the streams that feed the river Jordan. No doubt seeing how a deer, during a drought or from heated pursuit, pants for one of these streams reminds the psalmist of their own situation. They too are experiencing a time of spiritual drought, even of danger. For whatever reason, they find themselves alone, cut off from the temple in Jerusalem all those miles away. It is here during happier times they would join with everyone else in singing and shouting praise to God. Tragically, this is now but a painful memory.

No less than three times we read of their profound anguish, of their dislocation. It seems as if they have been swept away as by one of the powerful torrents crashing down the slopes of Mount Hermon, tossed about by the powerful currents.

Troubled by the taunts of their enemies, it seems that even God has forgotten them. But, of course, he hasn't. The very opposite, for even amid their turmoil the psalmist is confident that their deep yearning for God will be satisfied.

Whatever our situation, this psalm calls on us to resolve that,
come what may, we will place our full trust in God.
After all, he is our rock, as steadfast as any mountain.

ROSS MOUGHTIN

Dear divided church: 1 Corinthians

 As we come to the end of the Week of Prayer for Christian Unity (18–25 January), it is good to turn to a letter written to a chronically divided church. It is also fitting that the letter was written by the apostle Paul, whose conversion is marked on the final day of this week of prayer. Paul's meeting with Jesus and the new life he found in Christ are fundamental to him, as is the need for Christ's followers to find their unity as the body of Christ, serving and witnessing in the world.

The letter known as 1 Corinthians is part of an ongoing correspondence between Paul and the church that he had helped to found. Much of that correspondence has been lost, but what has been preserved, in the form of the two New Testament letters, gives a brilliant insight into Paul's thinking and his work with a Christian community as it develops its life and as relationships between church and apostle become strained. In his first visit to Corinth he had been nervous and unsure how to speak but had resolved to focus on Christ and above all Christ crucified. It is to this foundation that Paul returns again and again within the letter.

Jesus Christ, crucified and risen, is for Paul the heart of our faith, the reason for our hope and the inspirer of our love; it is these three gifts that abide, the greatest being love (1 Corinthians 13:13). It is Christ's love that binds Christians as one. This is why Paul is appalled by the divisions in the Corinthian church. Disunity had become focused around the different leaders – Paul, Peter and Apollos – with Christ himself taken by some as their party label. 'Has Christ been divided?' Paul asks in horror (1:13, NRSV). Other fault lines had developed too, centring around knowledge, social standing and wealth, attitudes to food, disagreements about marriage and sex, forms of public worship and church collections. Paul attempts to respond to all these disputes, always returning to that focus on Jesus Christ, the name he calls to mind in the very first and last sentences of this letter.

Let's delve into this great letter, wrestling with its challenges and letting it lead us to the crucified and risen one, Jesus Christ.

TERRY HINKS

Give thanks always

I give thanks to my God always for you because of the grace of God that has been given you in Christ Jesus, for in every way you have been enriched in him, in speech and knowledge of every kind.

It's not always easy to be thankful in life. Things go wrong or we mess up, and gratitude is squeezed out of our hearts and minds. We start to look at life resentfully or regretfully, rather than thankfully. Yet thanksgiving is at the heart of the Christian life – something underlined whenever we share in bread and wine (the thanksgiving meal), remembering how Jesus took those gifts, gave thanks to his Father (on the night of his betrayal and arrest) and gave them to his friends.

Paul always begins his letters with thanksgiving. In this he was in part simply following the custom of letter-writing in his day. The letters he wrote followed a standard structure – a habit that had become ingrained within him. Yet thankfulness was more than a habit for him; it flowed out of his experience of the grace of God in Christ Jesus. So when Paul writes to the church at Corinth, he first gives thanks for them, despite all the pain they are causing him. The letter will go on to address fundamental matters of faith and church order and confront divisions, injustices, distortions to the faith and failures to love, yet still Paul begins with thankfulness.

Above all Paul's gratitude focuses on what God has done and continues to do among and within the Corinthian Christians. It is that reality of overwhelming, amazing grace in his own life and theirs which keeps Paul thankful not just on the good days but always. It also keeps Paul from getting carried away with his own many gifts or overshadowed by those of the Corinthian Christians. Whatever gifts of speech or knowledge they may have are ultimately gifts from God, not reasons for arrogant pride. He turns the focus away from himself or the Corinthian church to the faithful God who has called all into fellowship with his Son, Jesus Christ.

*Give thanks to your God today, with a grateful heart,
humble mind and willing spirit.*

TERRY HINKS

Christ divided?

For it has been reported to me by Chloe's people that there are quarrels among you, my brothers and sisters. What I mean is that each of you says, 'I belong to Paul', or 'I belong to Apollos', or 'I belong to Cephas', or 'I belong to Christ.' Has Christ been divided? Was Paul crucified for you? Or were you baptised in the name of Paul?

Many of our soap operas thrive on people openly arguing with each other. None of the suppressed rage of the middle classes there; instead people tell it as it is and it's not always pleasant. Christian communities try to get along without such arguments, but every so often they break out with a vengeance. Once the genie is out of the bottle, it is very difficult to get it back in; the quarrels escalate and all too easily become personal.

This was certainly the case with the Corinthian church. Quarrels over different ways of presenting the faith, different tastes and habits, different personalities and backgrounds became focused on three key leaders who over the years had had a major influence on the church. Some looked to Peter, the fisherman who had followed Jesus from the earliest days. Others stood up for Paul, who had brought the gospel to the Corinthians and had given so much to build up the church. Others saw themselves as belonging to Apollos, the eloquent preacher who had helped strengthen the Christian movement in Corinth. Yet others saw themselves as above such factions and belonging to Christ himself.

In each case Paul uses the word 'I' to emphasise how the Christians in Corinth had forgotten their corporate belonging to Christ and made even Christ's name a divisive party slogan. Far from commending the group claiming to belong to Christ, he wants all to recognise that they belong to the Christ who had been crucified for them all. As for those seeing themselves as belonging to Paul himself, he will have nothing to do with them. The new birth of baptism isn't accomplished in his name. As he will write later in the same letter, 'For in the one Spirit we were all baptised into one body' (12:13).

Father, may your church be one in Christ, that the world may believe.

TERRY HINKS

The foolishness of God

For Jews demand signs and Greeks desire wisdom, but we proclaim Christ crucified, a stumbling-block to Jews and foolishness to Gentiles, but to those who are the called, both Jews and Greeks, Christ the power of God and the wisdom of God.

Who among us wants to be shown up as foolish? Who wants to admit to weakness, to needing help? Many of us will do virtually anything to prevent people seeing behind the strong, smiling mask. We want to be wise and in control. We want to be strong and independent, able to face anything life throws at us. We certainly want God to be these things – that ultimate rock we can depend upon, that ultimate force that will sort the mess out.

Yet Paul challenges us with a paradox: a God supremely revealed in what looks like weakness and folly. How can a man hanging limply from a cross, with blood dripping from his pierced hands, speak of an almighty God? In the Jewish tradition, such a death looked more like a sinner cursed by God than a Messiah and Saviour or a sign of God at work. For the Greek philosophers, such a messy death had nothing to say of that supreme passionless being – unmoved and unmoving – that they regarded as divine.

Paul would have felt the same, until an encounter with this Jesus of Nazareth, crucified and risen, turned his mind and his world upside down. From then on, the cross was his supreme reference point as he considered how to live and act day by day and as he explored the reality of God in a world of suffering and sin. As the chaplain Geoffrey Studdert-Kennedy wrote, in the face of the horrors of World War I, 'I do not know or love the Almighty potentate – my only real God is the suffering Father revealed in the sorrow of Christ' (*The Hardest Part*).

This is the God who Paul proclaims, and this is the God we need to know and love as we reach out to a needy world.

God of the cross, turn our minds and hearts to you, that we may know the power and wisdom of your love, in Christ Jesus.

TERRY HINKS

Spirit search

As it is written, 'What no eye has seen, nor ear heard, nor the human heart conceived, what God has prepared for those who love him' – these things God has revealed to us through the Spirit; for the Spirit searches everything, even the depths of God.

Paul continues his exploration of the wisdom of God shown in the apparent foolishness of the cross. He brings together some verses from Isaiah and Jeremiah to remind his readers that divine wisdom is beyond human comprehension and that we cannot domesticate God or limit the work of God. But then Paul proclaims that this mystery has been revealed by God through the work of God's Spirit among us. Thus the love of God connects with our love, the mind of Christ changes our minds and the Spirit of God transforms our spirits.

Paul is wrestling with deep things here, realities where we are all, as human beings, totally out of our depth. Humanity may be able to put a man on the moon, discover the intricacies of DNA, explore the depths of space and create artificial intelligence, but in terms of searching the depths of God, humanity on its own has no clue where to start. Human philosophies and natural theologies so easily get stuck in circular arguments, and the alternatives of agnosticism or atheism have little to offer in terms of going deeper into life. For Paul the depths of God are seen above all in the reality of the cross of Christ, the paradox of life given in death, love poured out, in the midst of hatred. These are the depths, but human minds cannot easily grasp this mystery. It requires God's life-giving Spirit to stir up and plumb these depths: the Spirit that stirs within God and stirs, by God's grace, within those open to the Spirit's workings.

The Spirit that searches the very depths of God is also the Spirit that searches our depths, showing us who we really are and who we might become, by the grace of God.

Come, Holy Spirit, come deep within us, taking us into the heart of God, opening us to the amazing grace of our Lord Jesus Christ.

TERRY HINKS

The Spirit lives in you

Do you not know that you are God's temple and that God's Spirit dwells in you? If anyone destroys God's temple, God will destroy that person. For God's temple is holy, and you are that temple.

The fire at Notre Dame on 15 April 2019 sent shockwaves through Paris, France and the world. No one was killed, unlike the brutal terrorist attacks in recent years, but even so there was an outpouring of grief and sympathy. Tears were shed, prayers were offered, money was pledged and the commitment to rebuild made within days. Like so many other churches, temples and sacred buildings, Notre Dame has a powerful place within the human imagination and psyche.

Paul no doubt also knew the power of buildings, for good and for ill. The sacred temple in Jerusalem still had a place in his heart, according to the picture given in Acts 21:26–27 (where Paul is spotted in the temple and arrested as a result). But in today's passage he takes the image of the sacred temple and applies it to the Christian community. It is this gathering of ordinary people – few of whom were wise by human standards, powerful or of noble birth (1 Corinthians 1:26) – which is the dwelling place for God's Spirit, the outpouring of God's love. And woe betide anyone who attempts to destroy that temple; they shall not succeed. There is an echo here of the words of Jesus to Peter in the gospels: 'On this rock I will build my church, and the gates of Hades will not prevail against it' (Matthew 16:18).

In the west, many of us, both inside and outside the church, have a jaded view of the institution of the church. The organisation seems to us to be all too human and fallible, weak and failing. Yet what might happen if we recaptured Paul's sense that the church, for all its weaknesses, is God's temple, a dwelling place for the Spirit to bring healing, hope, love and purpose to humanity as a whole?

Recognise the community of which you are part as a sacred space for God.
What difference does that make to you in your daily life?
Carry that gracious Spirit into every part of your life.

TERRY HINKS

Food, glorious food

Now concerning food sacrificed to idols: we know that 'all of us possess knowledge.' Knowledge puffs up, but love builds up. Anyone who claims to know something does not yet have the necessary knowledge; but anyone who loves God is known by him.

It is good to remember that we are reading a letter that is responding to concerns raised by a group of ordinary, fallible Christians. We don't have their letter, but it seems that at times Paul quotes phrases they have written or that have been reported to him. (This is not always easy to spot, as New Testament Greek doesn't have quotation marks.) Here Paul is probably quoting the Corinthians' remark that 'all of us possess knowledge'. This superior knowledge on the part of some of the Corinthians means that they feel they can eat food sacrificed to pagan idols without any danger, as they know that the idols have no real existence.

Paul knows this too, but he is not so quick to tuck in. What about those for whom the ancient pagan gods still seem to have some power – those who may waver as to the reality or otherwise of this multitude of alternatives to the living God? What if they see him enjoying a steak originally offered to Zeus? Might it not unsettle them?

Food has become a huge business in western society, with a multitude of restaurants serving food of every kind. Christians feel that we are free from the food regulations of the past or of other faiths. Yet we cannot eat without thought. There are always implications in what and how much we eat. The food miles spent on getting some out-of-season vegetable on to our plates; the conditions in which an animal was raised; the fact that many across the world do not have enough to eat, while we waste tonnes of food each year; the dependence of many in our own nation on food banks: these are all issues we cannot ignore. We cannot eat a mouthful without thinking through the implications of what we eat.

For Paul the real scandal in Corinth was how some would feast at the Lord's Supper and leave others with nothing. That scandal remains.

Loving Father, give to us all bread sufficient for the day.

TERRY HINKS

Training for life

Do you not know that in a race the runners all compete, but only one receives the prize? Run in such a way that you may win it. Athletes exercise self-control in all things; they do it to receive a perishable garland, but we an imperishable one.

Approaching the age of 60, I realise that I need to exercise more systematically than I have in past years. I can't just rely on the occasional good long walk or an afternoon in the garden. Too much of my time is spent in the car or in front of the computer, and I need to get out there, using my legs and my body; otherwise I fear I may stiffen and seize up. I'm not planning to enter a marathon or swim the Channel, but I need exercise.

Paul, like many of his contemporaries, enjoyed using the illustration of the athlete. Did he, I wonder, like going to see the Greek games (not something that had a big place within Jewish tradition)? He knows that he himself has been enrolled in a race of faith and hope. The love of God has claimed him for this race, with the prize of being with Christ and raised to new life with him at the end of the journey. The prize is not guaranteed. The race must be run fairly (no disqualifications) and with determination (no turning back).

The metaphor is not perfect: the race is a cooperative one rather than a competition, and there is not just one winner, be that an individual or a group. Rather the prize is there for all to reach out for and claim. But what Paul is trying to do is challenge the Corinthians' complacency. As Dietrich Bonhoeffer pointed out, the grace of God is free, but it is not cheap; there is a daily cost in following Christ, seeking God's kingdom and doing God's will.

We all need a bit of self-discipline to exercise and resist that cream cake. The business of discipleship is no different. The stakes are even higher, as we are looking to the health not simply of our bodies but of our very souls – our relationship to our God, to humanity and all creation.

Go on, get exercising! To the glory of God!

TERRY HINKS

Handed on to you

For I received from the Lord what I also handed on to you, that the Lord Jesus on the night when he was betrayed took a loaf of bread, and when he had given thanks, he broke it and said, 'This is my body that is for you. Do this in remembrance of me.'

This is the earliest known recording of what happened on the night Jesus was betrayed and led off to trial and execution, written by Paul some years before the earliest of the gospel accounts. As such, it is a set of words to be treasured and pondered upon. References to what Jesus had said and taught are few and far between in Paul's letter (though there are many more echoes of Jesus' teaching than may first appear). The scarcity of the words makes this passage all the more significant. Paul is reminding us of an action that helps define who we are as a Christian community. He is passing on a tradition that comes from Jesus himself, words and actions used and reused by the Christian community, traced back to a certain definable time and place.

Paul feels it necessary to remind the Corinthian Christians of this because of the abuses going on in that church – the divisions and lack of care that are all too apparent in the way they celebrate their meals together. The reference to the betrayal of Jesus may be there to challenge them to consider how they are betraying their Lord in the way they treat the poorer members of the community.

I imagine that for Paul, Jesus' words 'This is my body' refer not simply to the bread broken, but to the whole action of the community sharing food together. They connect very powerfully to Paul's image of the church community as the body of Christ – a body with many diverse parts, yet all joined by the Spirit and united in Christ.

These words and actions of Jesus have been passed on to our own generation of Christians. Will we live them out and pass them on to future generations? Will we be the body of Christ to those around us today?

Thank you, Lord, for all that we have received.
Help us to hand your grace on.

TERRY HINKS

One glorious body

For just as the body is one and has many members, and all the members of the body, though many, are one body, so it is with Christ. For in the one Spirit we were all baptised into one body – Jews or Greeks, slaves or free – and we were all made to drink of one Spirit.

Communication technology and social media have connected people in ways that were unimaginable in Paul's day. Events on the other side of the world impact us through our television, computer and phone screens. News flows 24/7. The opinions of bloggers, influencers and trolls touch us and challenge or reinforce our viewpoints. We have more information at our fingertips than ever before, yet we can feel overwhelmed by the sheer quantity (and variation in quality) of material and helpless to bring about change. Too often we feel like spectators, watching on as the car crash takes place, unable to help in any way. We cannot see the wood for the trees.

Paul had none of the advantages of communication that we have. His letters took weeks to arrive, carried by friends or fellow workers. Yet his sense of connection with Christians across the Mediterranean was incredibly deep and powerful, both to those he knew (like many in Corinth) and to those whom he had never met but had heard of through others. His journeys involved risk and hardship but were vital to him as a way of communicating his message and of meeting other Christians, though inevitably they could only be occasional.

He kept this connectedness through prayer, correspondence and a network of fellow missionaries, and above all his conviction that all are members of the one body of Christ, connected as organs and members of the same organism. The one baptism, one meal and one Spirit all united them in Christ, whatever their differences of race, background or situation. It meant that Paul could emphasise the needs of 'the many' and never retreat into some exclusive elite, 'the few'. That challenge remains for us: to look beyond 'the few', and those who are like us, to 'the many' in all their diversity, all made one in Christ.

Christ of all times, widen our vision of your body today.

TERRY HINKS

Love matters

If I speak in the tongues of mortals and of angels, but do not have love, I am a noisy gong or a clanging cymbal. And if I have prophetic powers, and understand all mysteries and all knowledge, and if I have all faith, so as to remove mountains, but do not have love, I am nothing.

Of all the writings of Paul, perhaps none is as familiar or as popular as 1 Corinthians 13. It has been read at countless weddings and many funerals too, treasured by Christians all over the world and down the centuries.

Yet this familiarity may obscure just how radical these words are. They challenge the view that Paul's message is all about being put right with God, through our faith. They, in fact, challenge the very words of Jesus, words that Paul no doubt knew (and treasured) and that some of the Corinthian Christians may have been using as their mantra. Paul picks up Jesus' phrase about a faith that can move mountains, but tells the wayward Corinthians that such faith is useless without love. Faith has immense eternal value, but ultimately it is subordinate to love – the love of God, shown in Christ, that we can trust utterly and the love that we are called to share and live by, as people of faith. Without that love we are nothing.

What a terrible self-discovery it would be to find that for all our skills and abilities, all our successes and achievements, all our knowledge and possessions, we are at heart 'nothing'. Pray to God that we can avoid that emptiness; pray that we can receive and give love in our lives; pray that God will teach us the way of love. We won't achieve this by our own efforts or abilities. Ultimately we will love because we have first been loved: loved by God in creation, loved by God in the redeeming work of Jesus Christ and loved by God in the continuing outpouring of the Holy Spirit. Allow that love in and life changes, blossoms, becomes fulfilled – we become 'someone', loved and loving.

God of all, open our lives this day to your love,
spoken so wonderfully through Jesus Christ.

TERRY HINKS

Infants and adults

I thank God that I speak in tongues more than all of you; nevertheless, in church I would rather speak five words with my mind, in order to instruct others also, than ten thousand words in a tongue. Brothers and sisters, do not be children in your thinking; rather, be infants in evil, but in thinking be adults.

In recent years there has been a tidal wave of popular opinion disillusioned with experts and intellectuals. In the church, too, there are those who have become suspicious of theologians and thinkers, unsure of the value of the intellect in the Christian journey. Belief and thought, religion and science have been seen by many as opposing forces, struggling for supremacy.

Paul, on the other hand, wants Christians to use their minds as well as their hearts, for them to grow and mature in their faith and not simply stay in the same place. In his great meditation on love (1 Corinthians 13), he talks of how he is putting childish ways behind him; he continues that theme as he discusses the place of speaking in tongues within the church's life. He himself prays in the Spirit and speaks in tongues in his praise of God, but his concern is above all for those who are still exploring the faith and seeking Christ, the stranger and newcomer at the church gatherings. How can we echo Paul's focus on the marginal and vulnerable, the seekers and those making the first steps of faith? How can we help those who need building up in their lives and their hope in God? The Spirit does not only warm hearts; the Spirit also stretches minds, enabling the gospel to be shared in new and vibrant ways.

We are called to love God not just with our hearts, but with our minds (and lives) too. Yes, we are to be like children in our openness and acceptance of God's kingdom, but we also need to grow up in Christ. Can we be infants in relation to evil but adults in terms of thinking, or, as Jesus put it, 'as shrewd as snakes and as innocent as doves' (Matthew 10:16, NIV)?

Help me, Lord, to put aside childish ways and to grow up in Christ, seeking always to live as your beloved child.

TERRY HINKS

First importance?

For I handed on to you as of first importance what I in turn had received: that Christ died for our sins in accordance with the scriptures, and that he was buried, and that he was raised on the third day in accordance with the scriptures, and that he appeared to Cephas, then to the twelve... Last of all, as to someone untimely born, he appeared also to me.

What is the most important thing you have learned in recent years? What is your main aim for today? What's your top priority for the months ahead? Past, present and the future, we all need to sort out our priorities, to sort out the wheat from the chaff, to know what is really crucial in life.

Priorities were something Jesus knew all about in his single-minded seeking of God's kingdom and fulfilling of God's will. Jesus' followers were challenged to sort out their priorities in the light of his death and resurrection, a reality that turned their worlds upside down. Paul makes it very clear that Christ's death and resurrection are fundamental; remove these and the good news ceases to be good or newsworthy.

The problem for us in the 21st century is that we are bombarded by so many messages that this one fundamental can be lost among the general noise, fake news and cheap promises. Why should it stand out among so many claims on our time, emotions and money? For Paul, the message made sense because of his own experience, his own encounter with the wounded, risen, glorious Christ. He knew himself forgiven, saved by Christ's death, called to follow and proclaim Jesus as Lord.

Can that be our priority and experience, too? Can our world be turned upside down by this new dawn? Yes, it can, as we give attention to the story handed on to us from one generation to another, as we meet Christ today in many different guises and as his story becomes our story, perhaps dramatically and suddenly or very gradually and gently. Then, like Paul, we will know what is 'of first importance'.

Ponder what is most important in your life.

TERRY HINKS

Victory day

'Death has been swallowed up in victory.' 'Where, O death, is your victory? Where, O death, is your sting?' The sting of death is sin, and the power of sin is the law. But thanks be to God, who gives us the victory through our Lord Jesus Christ. Therefore, my beloved, be steadfast, immovable, always excelling in the work of the Lord, because you know that in the Lord your labour is not in vain.

It's difficult for me to read these words without hearing the music of Handel's *Messiah*, a playful duet mocking death that leads on to the chorus, thanking God for the victory won through our Lord Jesus Christ. 'Thanks be to God' is repeated, again and again, words interweaving, rising and descending to express the wonder of what God has done in Christ.

The great theme of this passage is the victory God has won through Jesus Christ. His dying on the cross, his rising from the tomb, his living presence that cannot be defeated and his love from which we cannot be separated combine to vanquish the triple powers of death, sin and the demands of God's law, which together inflict despair, misery and guilt. The triple-wired cage that holds us is broken as we escape to new life, forgiven and free. The victory isn't simply God's and Christ's, glorious as that might be. For Paul it impacts our lives here and now – God gives *us* the victory that is Christ's.

That is why Christianity places thanksgiving at the heart of its faith and worship. It is our great hurrah to our victorious loving God. Thanksgiving for what God has done in Christ comes first; then and only then should we speak of work, service and good deeds. We are called to follow Christ, to work for God and to seek God's kingdom in prayer and action, knowing that God will bring all things to fruition and thankful that God is faithful to this promise. In the words of Julian of Norwich: 'All shall be well, and all shall be well, and all manner of thing shall be well.'

Thanks be to God for the victory Christ has won for me.

TERRY HINKS

Final word of love

All the brothers and sisters send greetings. Greet one another with a holy kiss. I, Paul, write this greeting with my own hand. Let anyone be accursed who has no love for the Lord. Our Lord, come! The grace of the Lord Jesus be with you. My love be with all of you in Christ Jesus.

How would you end a letter to a church that had caused you much heartache, but also was very dear to you? What would be your final words? Would you want to inspire or admonish? Warn or encourage?

After the stirring words of chapter 15 celebrating the victory of God in Christ, we may feel that the final chapter comes as something of an anticlimax. In it, Paul deals with practicalities about the collection being made for those in Judea affected by famine, speaks of arrangements for his possible visit, gives news about some of his fellow workers and ends with final greetings. Is this all too mundane?

We may want something more uplifting, but in fact we need these particular words to remind us what the Christian faith is all about. God doesn't simply give promises for the future; God is at work here and now – seen in the compassion shown for those in need, the faithfulness of real, fallible followers of Jesus and the many relationships of mutual care that grow up in the church and beyond. Love is not abstract but practical, and Paul repeats his plea: 'Let all that you do be done in love' (16:14).

It is love that is Paul's parting word. Taking the pen in his own hand, he adds his own greeting, written proof that he is author of the letter. He shares the grace of the Lord Jesus, as he does at the end of many of his letters, but then adds a personal assurance of his love for this troublesome church. Formulas are left behind as he speaks of his continuing love for them, a love that is inspired and renewed daily by his experience of Christ Jesus. Take that as Paul's word to you for today and live it.

Let the final word be love – our love for one another and for God, modelled on and moulded by the love of Christ.

TERRY HINKS

Esther

If, like me until recently, your knowledge of the book of Esther is largely limited to a vague memory of a beautiful queen and a pastry called Haman's ears, then you are in for a bit of a surprise. This book is full of energy, excitement, violence and danger. It contains a beautiful woman, an evil courtier, a subjugated people and a king – all elements that make for a most magnificent tale. But, of course, it is more than that; it is a powerful demonstration of courage and faith, intended to kindle the dying spark of hope which lay in the hearts of a crushed and persecuted people, bringing to flame a trust in God and his good purposes for his children.

The strange thing is that the book of Esther contains no actual mention of God at all! There are no references to the promised land, the law and the prophets or the holy city, Jerusalem. It seems as if this book is not religious at all; the only thing linking it to the rest of the Bible is the salvation of God's chosen people. And yet, although the Jewish people are threatened with annihilation, they survive. Although Esther must risk her life and the life of her people, she yet finds the courage to face King Xerxes. Although Mordecai is daily faced with persecution, he maintains his moral code and alerts the king to a plot to destroy him. Through all the events of this tumultuous book, God's presence, though unacknowledged, is clearly perceptible, as slowly and carefully he works through his people for their good.

Not all the book is an easy read – some passages are difficult and challenge our way of thinking about God's saving action. But we were never promised simplicity, and some of the moral dilemmas of this book are as relevant today as they were thousands of years ago. How to survive in difficult times; how to negotiate dangerous political situations; when to admit to one's faith and when to conceal it: all these are offered for our reflection. Some conundrums remain just that – moral challenges with no easy answer. But always the love of God for his people can be glimpsed just beneath the surface for those who would look deeper.

SALLY WELCH

A silent tongue

But Esther had kept secret her family background and nationality just as Mordecai had told her to do, for she continued to follow Mordecai's instructions as she had done when he was bringing her up.

One of the first decisions a newly ordained deacon in the Church of England has to make is whether to wear a 'dog collar' and, if so, how often. There are advantages to sporting a clerical collar – you don't have to explain why you greet everyone you pass; you don't take people by surprise when they discover what you do; you are allowed in places you might not otherwise gain entry to. On the other hand, the person who is visibly a priest gets loaded down with all sorts of assumptions and expectations of behaviour, which can obscure the real personality and character of the wearer. People who wear crosses around their necks or on lapels might find themselves similarly burdened by the prejudices of others – or even face active scorn and hostility. Declaring your faith openly can be a courageous act; it can even be a mission opportunity, as it can be a powerful conversation starter. But there are also times and places when to be openly Christian is foolhardy or even dangerous.

Esther is in such a situation – to be Jewish in the land of the Medes and Persians under the reign of the stern and all-powerful Xerxes was to run all sorts of risks. It would certainly have put her beyond the pale when it came to being chosen as one of the king's new concubines – and if it were to be discovered that she had deceived the king in such a way, her life would be in peril. So Esther keeps quiet, obediently following the instruction of her wise uncle who had brought her up.

There are times when we need to take our courage in both hands and declare our faith, to stand up for what we believe. There are other times, however, when we need to remain silent for the present, so that more good can be done in the future. Discerning those times takes great wisdom.

Spirit of truth and wisdom, give me the grace to choose rightly when to speak and when to remain silent.

SALLY WELCH

Pride and prejudice

After these events, King Xerxes honoured Haman son of Hammedatha, the Agagite, elevating him and giving him a seat of honour higher than that of all the other nobles. All the royal officials at the king's gate knelt down and paid honour to Haman, for the king had commanded this concerning him. But Mordecai would not kneel down or pay him honour… When Haman saw that Mordecai would not kneel down or pay him honour, he was enraged. Yet having learned who Mordecai's people were, he scorned the idea of killing only Mordecai. Instead Haman looked for a way to destroy all Mordecai's people, the Jews, throughout the whole kingdom of Xerxes.

Haman is a man to whom status and power are all-important. It really matters to him not only that he has achieved the position he has, but also that all those around him should acknowledge this. And how vicious is Haman to those who refuse to give him the respect he believes he deserves. Not just Mordecai is going to be made to suffer – no, this is not enough for a man whose dignity has been upset, who feels disrespected! Many must feel the consequences of Mordecai's refusal to honour Haman.

How many times do we encounter people like this in our daily lives – people who feel they deserve to be treated in a certain way because of how much wealth they have or what they have achieved? And we see that in their turn they give value only to the wealthy or important, the powerful and successful. If we are honest with ourselves, are there occasions when we make assumptions about a person's worth based solely on how much money they have or what they have achieved? Do we genuinely respect the homeless person as much as the owner of the chain of supermarkets in whose doorway they are sheltering? Is the groundsman admired as much as the top-league footballer who plays on the perfectly mown turf?

Ask God for the grace to live out Jesus' injunction: 'Whoever wants to become great among you must be your servant, and whoever wants to be first must be your slave' (Matthew 20:26–27).

SALLY WELCH

Seeds of hatred

Then Haman said to King Xerxes, 'There is a certain people dispersed among the peoples in all the provinces of your kingdom who keep themselves separate. Their customs are different from those of all other people, and they do not obey the king's laws; it is not in the king's best interest to tolerate them. If it pleases the king, let a decree be issued to destroy them, and I will give ten thousand talents of silver to the king's administrators for the royal treasury.'

How cleverly does Haman fasten on to the king's fears and insecurities to achieve his own ends! How subtle are the ways in which he points out the 'dangers' of the Jewish people, reinforcing prejudice and stirring up hatred. Haman tells the king that the Jewish people do not join in with the rest of the nation and that they have different customs – by implication scorning the customs of the king and his people. He cleverly works to build up fear, uncertainty and doubt until the king will agree to any measures in order to destroy this threat to his kingdom: 'It is not in the king's best interest to tolerate them.' I am reminded of the serpent's beguiling speeches in the garden of Eden, as poor Eve is tricked and flattered into committing that first great sin (Genesis 3:1–5).

The greatest crimes grow from the smallest of beginnings – perception of difference can lead imperceptibly to an assumption that difference is somehow bad. From there can come the belief that this 'bad' must be removed or destroyed.

We must be alert to the dangers of prejudice and to the possibility that we are making decisions based on false assumptions or have allowed others to influence us unjustly for their own ends. Our God bids us to take no notice of difference, but to welcome all, regardless of gender, race or creed. As former UN Secretary-General Kofi Annan said: 'Ignorance and prejudice are the handmaidens of propaganda. Our mission, therefore, is to confront ignorance with knowledge, bigotry with tolerance and isolation with the outstretched hand of generosity.'

Lord God, help me to do what is required of me: 'to act justly and to love mercy and to walk humbly with your God' (Micah 6:8).

SALLY WELCH

Annihilation

Dispatches were sent by couriers to all the king's provinces with the order to destroy, kill and annihilate all the Jews – young and old, women and children – on a single day, the thirteenth day of the twelfth month, the month of Adar, and to plunder their goods. A copy of the text of the edict was to be issued as law in every province and made known to the people of every nationality so that they would be ready for that day.

What a truly horrific passage this is! How it emphasises the completeness of the slaughter which is to come in the threefold order of destruction. Different translations use different words – slay, massacre, eliminate – but all include the triple pounding of an entire people into nothingness. King Xerxes has been seduced by the evil vanity of Haman, and now his entire kingdom will echo with the cries of men, women and children as they perish. To make matters worse, the day of annihilation has been appointed in the future – this is no spontaneous eruption of violence but a calculated act of cruelty as an innocent people are forced to wait helplessly for their death.

Our world today echoes with similar times of trauma and pain, as peoples, communities, families and individuals are singled out for their differences and the innocent are punished. It is easy to drown in feelings of hopelessness when faced with such mass suffering, to feel that there is no good in the world and possibly no God, if such an almighty being can allow evil to flourish in this way. But our faith is one of hope and love, even in the darkest times. The light of Christ shines in the darkness 'and the darkness has not overcome it' (John 1:5). It is our task both to keep that light alive in our hearts and to share that light among others, so that they too may have hope in times of darkness. Small acts of kindness and gestures of sympathy and love may not seem much in the tidal face of evil, but many small acts of love will prevent the darkness from engulfing the world.

'In him was life, and the life was the light of all people' (John 1:4, NRSV).

SALLY WELCH

'For such a time as this'

When Esther's words were reported to Mordecai, he sent back this answer: 'Do not think that because you are in the king's house you alone of all the Jews will escape. For if you remain silent at this time, relief and deliverance for the Jews will arise from another place, but you and your father's family will perish. And who knows but that you have come to your royal position for such a time as this?'

Esther has told Mordecai that she cannot plead on their people's behalf because she hasn't been before the king for a while. This is Mordecai's response. Just as there was a time for Esther to hide her origins, now it is time that she steps forward and risks everything. Mordecai reminds her that she is part of the bigger picture and that her obligations extend far beyond saving her own life. But even this must be of her own free will. For Mordecai is in no doubt that, if Esther does nothing, 'relief and deliverance for the Jews will arise from another place'. He believes that God will save his children in some way, but he is asking Esther to choose rightly – to allow herself to be the instrument of that salvation.

We all have moments of decision in our lives – moments when we can choose to do what we know in our hearts to be the good action or to speak out against what we believe to be wrong. Equally, we can ignore the call to justice or love, preferring instead to hide amid selfishness and cruelty, hard-heartedness or neglect. If we are open to his prompting, God will work in us and through us, impelling us towards the best choice. But always he will leave it to us to make the final decision – that is his gift and his grace.

And with every choice, our words and actions are woven together to become threads in the cloth of the story of the human race – threads that can be pure gold, enhancing the pattern of salvation, or dirty and corrupt, soiling the fabric of creation.

---

*Heavenly Father, help me to listen to your promptings
so that I may respond rightly.*

SALLY WELCH

'If I perish, I perish'

Then Esther sent this reply to Mordecai: 'Go, gather together all the Jews who are in Susa, and fast for me. Do not eat or drink for three days, night or day. I and my attendants will fast as you do. When this is done, I will go to the king, even though it is against the law. And if I perish, I perish.'

Yesterday we heard Mordecai's challenge; today we read of Esther's response. She has hidden her identity, her faith, for many years, taking on the ways of another people, hiding her true self so that she might survive. But today she puts all that aside – all the subterfuge and deception, the excuses and denial. She will face up to what is right and accept the consequences. But she cannot do this by herself – perhaps, after so many years of hiding, she does not feel familiar enough with her faith practices; perhaps she needs the support of knowing that many people are praying with her and for her as she walks boldly into danger. So she gathers her people around her, to encourage her and pray with her so that even as she takes those final steps towards her fate, she knows she is not alone.

What a wonderful affirmation of the power of a praying community! When Esther enters the court of the king, she will be surrounded by the prayers of her people. Do our churches behave in the same way today? Are they communities of encouragement and support? Is there a way in which we as individuals can build up others through our prayers and worship? Simply letting others know you are praying for them can be a very powerful source of comfort. And it works both ways – a woman I know keeps a prayer diary in which she writes all her prayer requests over the weeks and years. She says it gives her enormous hope and encouragement when she looks back to see how her prayers have been answered – not perhaps in the way that she expected or hoped, but always for the good.

Almighty and all-powerful God, help me to be a prayer warrior, empowering others to face their challenges with courage and hope.

SALLY WELCH

No satisfaction

Haman went out that day happy and in high spirits. But when he saw Mordecai at the king's gate and observed that he neither rose nor showed fear in his presence, he was filled with rage against Mordecai. Nevertheless, Haman restrained himself and went home. Calling together his friends and Zeresh, his wife, Haman boasted to them about his vast wealth, his many sons, and all the ways the king had honoured him and how he had elevated him above the other nobles and officials. 'And that's not all,' Haman added. 'I'm the only person Queen Esther invited to accompany the king to the banquet she gave. And she has invited me along with the king tomorrow. But all this gives me no satisfaction as long as I see that Jew Mordecai sitting at the king's gate.'

It is a truism that a person who owns the only car in a road full of bicycle-owners feels rich, while a person who owns a Rolls Royce in a street full of private-jet-owners feels poor. In other words, how wealthy or fortunate we feel with our lot in life depends largely on whom we compare ourselves with. Haman clearly suffers from extreme envy – not satisfied with his wealth, his sons and all the honours he has received, he feels that in order to be truly rich he must witness the downfall of his bitter enemy, Mordecai.

We all have a tendency to compare ourselves with those who are better off than we are, rather than those whose life circumstances are more challenging. Today, let us be thankful for where we live, what we have eaten, the people we have talked to, the things we have read or heard and the opportunities for leisure we have had. Let us pray for those who lack some or all of these things.

Reflect: if you have food in your fridge, clothes on your body, a roof over your head and a place to sleep, you're richer than 75% of the entire world.

SALLY WELCH

Comeuppance!

When Haman entered, the king asked him, 'What should be done for the man the king delights to honour?' Now Haman thought to himself, 'Who is there that the king would rather honour than me?' So he answered the king, 'For the man the king delights to honour, have them bring a royal robe the king has worn and a horse the king has ridden, one with a royal crest placed on its head. Then let the robe and horse be entrusted to one of the king's most noble princes. Let them robe the man the king delights to honour, and lead him on the horse through the city streets, proclaiming before him, "This is what is done for the man the king delights to honour!"' 'Go at once,' the king commanded Haman. 'Get the robe and the horse and do just as you have suggested for Mordecai the Jew, who sits at the king's gate. Do not neglect anything you have recommended.'

The writer of the book of Esther must have thoroughly enjoyed this part of the story. All this time the wickedness of Haman has been gradually revealed. He is seen as hard-hearted and envious, selfish and boastful, lacking the most basic of empathy for his fellow human beings. He is all about looking after number one – and it seems as if his moment has come. How we smile as we anticipate Haman's reaction to the king's commandments. How Haman must have struggled to control his expression as all the honours that he anticipated are to be heaped on his most bitter enemy – and he is the one who must undertake the task!

Here at last is the beginning of the story of reversal that is at the heart of the book of Esther. God, though hidden, has not been inactive. But this is no deus ex machina in action – no lightning-bolt operation. Mordecai himself, by his just and brave actions, first set things in motion; he is simply being finally rewarded for his loyalty to the king, the action of a good citizen.

Father, help me to remember that mine 'are the hands with which God is to bless his people' (Teresa of Avila).

SALLY WELCH

The deciding moment

So the king and Haman went to Queen Esther's banquet, and as they were drinking wine on the second day, the king again asked, 'Queen Esther, what is your petition? It will be given you. What is your request? Even up to half the kingdom, it will be granted.' Then Queen Esther answered, 'If I have found favour with you, Your Majesty, and if it pleases you, grant me my life – this is my petition. And spare my people – this is my request. For I and my people have been sold to be destroyed, killed and annihilated. If we had merely been sold as male and female slaves, I would have kept quiet, because no such distress would justify disturbing the king.'

This is it, then: the climax of the book of Esther; the part which we hear about in lectionaries; the moment which is acted out in Sunday clubs and activity sessions. It is here that Esther puts her life on the line to plead for her people. If she is wrong – if she has not prepared properly or if she has misjudged the moment – then not only she but every Jewish person under the reign of King Xerxes will lose their lives. It is a moment of high drama, made more so by Esther's repetition of the threefold death sentence 'destroyed, killed and annihilated' used in the original edict.

Not every deciding moment is so easy to identify. They may slip by almost unnoticed as we decide to walk past a person in distress; not to call upon a neighbour who is new to the area, sick or bereaved; not to apologise to someone we know we have hurt; not to offer to help a person, group or community. But they build up, these moments, until they are in danger of defining our lives by their selfishness or thoughtlessness. Only with constant watchfulness will we be able to walk the path of righteousness – that and God's unending grace.

'We can do no great things – only small things with great love'
(Mother Teresa of Calcutta).

SALLY WELCH

Reversal

The king's edict granted the Jews in every city the right to assemble and protect themselves; to destroy, kill and annihilate the armed men of any nationality or province who might attack them and their women and children, and to plunder the property of their enemies… On the thirteenth day of the twelfth month, the month of Adar, the edict commanded by the king was to be carried out. On this day the enemies of the Jews had hoped to overpower them, but now the tables were turned and the Jews got the upper hand over those who hated them.

Tomorrow we will be looking further at the issues of mass slaughter – today, we will simply celebrate the reversal of fortune of the Jewish subjects of King Xerxes, who for some time had been living with the certain knowledge that on the 'thirteenth day of the twelfth month' they would be put to death by order of the king.

To hear that the shadow of death has been removed from an entire people is a matter of great rejoicing. Parallels of God's saving action in Christ must surely resonate with us at this point. Mary's great song in response to the imminent birth of her child celebrates a world in which those at the bottom of the heap are raised up above their oppressors: 'He has performed mighty deeds with his arm; he has scattered those who are proud in their inmost thoughts. He has brought down rulers from their thrones but has lifted up the humble' (Luke 1:51–52). Despite the apparent absence of God from the story of Esther and her people, we see his saving hand at work – surely a message of hope for those who were living as 'strangers in a strange land', as many Jewish people were at the time this book was written.

And what of us? Do we have hope that God is still at work even though we cannot perceive his presence? Are we reassured that in Christ's kingdom, all will be equal and to all who seek mercy, mercy will be granted? We should be, for so we have been promised.

'My soul glorifies the Lord and my spirit rejoices in God my Saviour'
(Luke 1:46–47).

SALLY WELCH

Revenge or justice?

The Jews struck down all their enemies with the sword, killing and destroying them, and they did what they pleased to those who hated them. In the citadel of Susa, the Jews killed and destroyed five hundred men. They also killed Parshandatha, Dalphon, Aspatha, Poratha, Adalia, Aridatha, Parmashta, Arisai, Aridai and Vaizatha, the ten sons of Haman son of Hammedatha, the enemy of the Jews. But they did not lay their hands on the plunder.

Unsurprisingly, this part of the story of Esther is usually missed out in sermons and Bible studies. However, we would be doing the compilers of the canon of scripture an injustice if we did not try to understand the significance of this chapter, and the reasons behind the actions of the Jewish people. There isn't enough space in this reflection for deep enquiry, but it is worth considering the following points.

First, although expressly allowed to 'plunder the property of their enemies' (8:11), they did not do so. Three times we are told this (9:10, 15–16). This reminds us that the slaughter is not for financial gain or personal advancement. Again, their violence is presented as defensive and justified – the Jewish people are only responding to the threat upon their own lives by 'those who hated them'. This response is measured and equal – fulfilling the Old Testament requirements of 'an eye for an eye' (Exodus 21:23–25). There is the further consideration that if these aggressors were not put to death, what then should happen to them? They could not all be imprisoned, and if left free might pose a constant and perpetual danger.

However, in Christian eyes, all these arguments are rebutted in the words of Christ: 'You have heard that it was said, "Eye for eye, and tooth for tooth." But I tell you, do not resist an evil person. If anyone slaps you on the right cheek, turn to them the other cheek also' (Matthew 5:38–39). Of such complicated, moral quandaries is our daily life made up – not always life-or-death situations but nonetheless ones that we must consider carefully, looking always for the truth, the righteousness and the will of God within.

Lord, help me to act with mercy and justice, with love in my heart.

SALLY WELCH

Purim

That is why rural Jews – those living in villages – observe the fourteenth of the month of Adar as a day of joy and feasting, a day for giving presents to each other. Mordecai recorded these events, and he sent letters to all the Jews throughout the provinces of King Xerxes, near and far, that they should celebrate annually the fourteenth and fifteenth days of the month of Adar as the time when the Jews got relief from their enemies, and as the month when their sorrow was turned into joy and their mourning into a day of celebration. He wrote to them to observe the days as days of feasting and joy and giving presents of food to one another and gifts to the poor.

The feast of Purim (from the word for 'lots') celebrates the reversal of fortunes of the Jewish people in the kingdom of Xerxes. It is so called as Haman cast lots to determine the day of the slaughter – the day on which the Jewish people then turned the tables on Haman.

It is interesting to note that even before Mordecai authorised the day as a festival, celebration was already taking place at that time. Thus will a wise ruler sense the mood of their people and engage with it, regularising it in order to put it to good use – note how the people do not only feast but give 'presents to each other and gifts to the poor'. So is the rhythm of life honoured and made more profound – after a time of anguish and fear come joy and celebration; after bloodshed comes charity. The feast also marks a return to normality, as it ends the time of violence which, like all acts of aggression, might have become more intense and lengthy.

What is the message for us contemporary Christians? A deeper under-standing of the importance of festivals, perhaps; a reminder that cele-brations, sabbath times, are vital to the spiritual and emotional health of a people, a community. Perhaps too this is a reminder that there is a season for everything, and God's hand, although not always evident, is always present.

'To every thing there is a season, and a time to every purpose under the heaven' (Ecclesiastes 3:1, KJV).

SALLY WELCH

Remembering

So Queen Esther, daughter of Abihail, along with Mordecai the Jew, wrote with full authority to confirm this second letter concerning Purim. And Mordecai sent letters to all the Jews in the 127 provinces of Xerxes's kingdom – words of goodwill and assurance – to establish these days of Purim at their designated times, as Mordecai the Jew and Queen Esther had decreed for them, and as they had established for themselves and their descendants in regard to their times of fasting and lamentation. Esther's decree confirmed these regulations about Purim, and it was written down in the records.

Events which happen at festivals often stand out clearly in our memories, providing benchmarks throughout our lives. We can look back to the same festival year after year, using them to measure growth and change – the arrival and departure of family and friends, and changes of jobs, partners or houses. 'This time last year I was…' is a common phrase at birthdays and holidays, giving us firm anchor points in the sea of everyday living.

The wise Queen Esther and her adviser Mordecai are determined that God's saving action should not be lost or forgotten among the minutiae of normal life. It is easy to forget to count our blessings or to remember single acts of kindness when we are surrounded by the busyness of earning a living or simply getting through the day. This will not happen here – the festival of Purim is to take place every year, the story told, the gifts given. The dramatic turnaround of the fortunes of the Jewish people, living in exile under King Xerxes, will be a highlight in their history, reminding them that even if it seems God has deserted them, all the time his purposes are being worked out.

Should we perhaps make our own calendar of feast days? Should we write down occasions when we have clearly perceived God in action, noting the event and the date, so that we can look back in one year, five years and remember? It would perhaps give us hope in our darkest times and remind us that even if the sun isn't shining, that doesn't mean it isn't there.

Heavenly Father, help me always to remember your love.

SALLY WELCH

What would Jesus do?

Mordecai the Jew was second in rank to King Xerxes, pre-eminent among the Jews, and held in high esteem by his many fellow Jews, because he worked for the good of his people and spoke up for the welfare of all the Jews.

In the 1990s in America, a catchphrase developed among Christian youth groups and missions – 'What would Jesus do?', or WWJD. The roots of this phrase can be traced as far back as Augustine in the fourth century, who offered reflections on how to imitate Jesus' life. This idea was developed over the centuries, and in his influential book *The Imitation of Christ*, the 15th-century author Thomas à Kempis gave detailed instructions on how to live as Jesus would. Today my own diocese of Oxford has 'Called to be Christ-like' as its slogan – surely a 21st-century take on WWJD. All these phrases help to remind us of the presence of God and to reinforce our calling to follow Christ wherever we are, whatever we do. Although 'invisible', God's presence is thus constantly felt.

So, too, for the book of Esther. Although the name of God is not mentioned anywhere in this book, nonetheless his presence is clearly felt. It is through following God's law that Mordecai brings Esther up to be faithful and full of prayer. It is by calling upon her community of faith that Esther gains the courage to ask Xerxes to deliver her people. It is through remembering their religious obligations that the Jewish people limit their desire for vengeance and live peacefully within the kingdom afterwards.

'What would Jesus do?' may seem like a trite phrase, tripping easily off the tongue, barely skimming the surface of the complex and highly developed nature of our Christian faith. Nonetheless, it is a useful guide for busy times, a simple check when we are considering a speech or an action.

The rhyming may be trite, but the sentiment is useful:
If the sinful ways of life
You are tempted to pursue,
Just stop and think before you yield –
What would Jesus do? (D.O. Teasley, 1911)

SALLY WELCH

The four last things: death

I lived for several years in Berlin during the Cold War, in the shadow of the infamous Berlin Wall. Back then, West Berlin was an urban island in the middle of the former East Germany. Once half of a thriving capital city, with links all over Germany, it was then a truncated community, severed from its hinterland.

As in any city, many of its streets, bridges and metro stations were named for the places they had once led to – places now inaccessible and largely unknown to a whole generation of Berliners. Imagine, for instance, living in Sheffield, where I grew up, and seeing signs like Chesterfield Road but not having any idea where Chesterfield was or what it might be like there; this is how it was in Berlin. Whichever way you went, every metro line, every bus route and every street came up against a solid, immovable barrier. The end of the line.

Death feels like this: the end of the line. There may be hints and guesses as to what comes next, but nobody knows. It is beyond our experience.

But then the day dawned that nobody expected: the Berlin Wall came down, and the country was reunified. The first time I travelled through those apparently impassable barriers into all the surprises that lay beyond them, I was like a child in a candy store. It was such a joy to discover that the equivalent of all the Chesterfield Roads actually led to real, living Chesterfields, where people lived and loved, laughed and cried, and human life was lived to the full in ways that no street sign could have indicated.

I remember thinking that maybe death is like this. What if death isn't the end of the line, but the mystery that leads us beyond the signposts we now see into the living eternal reality to which they point?

I invite you, during the next two weeks, to explore something of what death means for you. We will look at some of the ways in which we experience the reality of our mortality, but we will also look beyond 'the end of the line' as we reflect on the glimpses scripture gives us of what lies beyond the horizon of our mortal vision.

MARGARET SILF

Time to move on

The Lord our God spoke to us at Horeb, saying, 'You have stayed long enough at this mountain. Resume your journey, and go into the hill country of the Amorites as well as into the neighbouring regions – the Arabah, the hill country, the Shephelah, the Negeb, and the sea coast – the land of the Canaanites and the Lebanon, as far as the great river, the river Euphrates. See, I have set the land before you; go in and take possession of the land that I swore to your ancestors.'

Death wears many guises. It comes to us in the dying of our hopes, dreams and ambitions. It comes stealthily as the years chip away at our energies, or it comes suddenly, overturning in an instant all that we thought we had built up.

Life gives us any number of dress rehearsals for death. This should not dismay us but rather be a cause for gratitude, because they invite us to sit more lightly to what is not eternal, cherishing the gifts of creation while we have them but recognising that they can be taken from us. Many people experience a significant 'death rehearsal', for example, in bereavement or when their children leave home. Perhaps the loss of job security, a relationship breakdown or a serious health issue breaks through our fragile defences. All of these life events are, in their own way, echoing the call of God in today's reading, to continue our journey, because we 'have stayed long enough at this mountain'.

It's time to move on, says God, and to resume the journey. What we think is the end is, in God's eyes, just the beginning of a new chapter. The call is to trust that death, whether of our dreams or our bodies, is more like climbing over a stile into a new form of life we can't even begin to imagine. Scripture expresses this in terms of the unknown territories waiting to be conquered, but for us the territory we are asked to conquer is our fear of climbing over that stile, however hard and painful that might be, trusting God for all that lies beyond our mortal vision.

What the caterpillar thinks is the end, for the butterfly is just the beginning.

MARGARET SILF

Not extinction, but transformation

Listen, I will tell you a mystery! We will not all die, but we will all be changed, in a moment, in the twinkling of an eye, at the last trumpet. For the trumpet will sound, and the dead will be raised imperishable, and we will be changed… When this perishable body puts on imperishability, and this mortal body puts on immortality, then the saying that is written will be fulfilled: 'Death has been swallowed up in victory. Where, O death, is your victory? Where, O death, is your sting?'

In her book *Water Bugs and Dragonflies*, Doris Stickney captures the heart of this 'mystery' of which Paul speaks, in a story to help young children understand how death is not an end but a new beginning. The water bugs are puzzled, because every so often one of them disappears beyond the water surface. They decide that the next time this happens the one who has disappeared will return to tell the others what is happening, but of course this is impossible, because once a water bug has passed through the boundary of the water surface it becomes a dragonfly and can never return. It has not died, but has been changed, in a moment, in the twinkling of an eye, into a very different form of life.

Shakespeare expresses this same mystery in Ariel's song in *The Tempest*. The song seeks to reassure Ferdinand, who believes his father has been drowned, that his father's bones are transforming into coral and his eyes into pearls: 'Nothing of him that doth fade, but doth suffer a sea-change into something rich and strange.'

When winter arrives, and life on earth slows down and dies back, we know that in the springtime it will emerge again, bringing forth a whole new season of life. Scripture echoes this truth over and over, assuring us, as in Paul's words today, that death is never extinction, but always transformation. I remember the day when this mystery became a living reality for me, the day I asked myself: 'In the light of this universal pattern of transformation, how could humankind possibly be an exception?'

May we move beyond the fear of death's sting to welcome the promise of transformation that it holds out to us.

MARGARET SILF

Love abides

Love never ends. But as for prophecies, they will come to an end; as for tongues, they will cease; as for knowledge, it will come to an end. For we know only in part, and we prophesy only in part; but when the complete comes, the partial will come to an end... For now we see in a mirror, dimly, but then we will see face to face. Now I know only in part; then I will know fully, even as I have been fully known. And now faith, hope, and love abide, these three; and the greatest of these is love.

If you have ever seen an ultrasound scan of an unborn child, you will probably have had considerable difficulty in identifying anything that looks remotely like a baby. In later pregnancy it becomes possible for a trained eye to determine the gender of the baby, but even a very late 3D scan bears scant resemblance to the child you will soon hold in your arms, let alone the grown person that child has the potential to become.

Paul recognises that creation is engaged in a process of birthing the new creation that God is dreaming into being. He reminds us today in powerful terms that what we now know and understand is as far from the fullness of all that shall be as a prenatal scan is from the reality of the fully mature person.

As we look towards the ending of our own lives or grieve for the loss of a loved one, we would be wise to reflect on this truth: that the life we regard as lost was just the early, still-unformed image of the fullness of all it shall be, just the brief trailer for an adventure into a life we cannot yet imagine. Grief will obscure our vision, but love is the key that unlocks this deep truth. All the love we have given and received is indestructible. It's the golden thread that binds our partial earthly life to our complete eternal life. Love never dies. Love grows. Love alone abides.

---

*As we look into the mirror today, may we catch a glimpse
not only of who we are but of all we shall become.*

MARGARET SILF

The grain that must die

Jesus answered them, 'The hour has come for the Son of Man to be glori-fied. Very truly, I tell you, unless a grain of wheat falls into the earth and dies, it remains just a single grain; but if it dies, it bears much fruit... Whoever serves me must follow me, and where I am, there will my ser-vant be also. Whoever serves me, the Father will honour. Now my soul is troubled. And what should I say – "Father, save me from this hour"? No, it is for this reason that I have come to this hour.'

Today we stand in prayer alongside Jesus as he faces the reality of his own imminent and brutal death, and listen as he reminds us of the unpalatable but undeniable truth about the grain of wheat that has to die if it is to live. This is such an obvious fact of nature, but one we rarely apply to ourselves. For every seed, this is the very nature of its life cycle: first it lives its one single life on earth, then it dies and is buried in the cold soil, and only then can it multiply and bring forth abundant fruit. Every seed holds the poten-tial of an entire harvest. Every acorn holds the potential of an entire oak forest. But these fruits are only possible if the single seed first disintegrates in death. Death is the catalyst for germination, the only way in which all the potential, dormant in the seed, can be brought to life.

How could it be otherwise for ourselves? Jesus tells us clearly that if we would follow him into the fullness of life, we must first follow him through the apparent emptiness and finality of death. Like his, our souls will also be troubled as we approach the reality of our earthly ending. Like him, we will beg to be spared the fateful hour. Can we also, like him, come to understand and accept that far from being the end of all we thought we were, this hour we so dread is the way, and the only way, to pass into all we are called to become?

May we learn to trust that death is not the enemy,
but the enabler of new life.

MARGARET SILF

Hand in hand with love

Do not fear, for I have redeemed you; I have called you by name, you are mine. When you pass through the waters, I will be with you; and through the rivers, they shall not overwhelm you; when you walk through fire you shall not be burned, and the flame shall not consume you. For I am the Lord your God, the Holy One of Israel, your Saviour… You are precious in my sight and honoured, and I love you… Do not fear, for I am with you.

Our reflections over the past two days have taught us two crucial truths as we face our own mortality: first, Jesus too trembled in dread as he faced the ending of his earthly life; second, love is the power that underpins all life and binds our earthly existence to our eternal life. In today's reading these two truths are combined into the promise that takes us beyond fear to trust: 'I am with you, and I love you.' Perhaps this is the bottom line of our faith: do we trust that God walks with us through the valley of the shadow of death, and do we trust in this promise of God's unfailing love?

On the face of it, the evidence of our earthly experience is not convincing. People die in dreadful, and sometimes avoidable, conflagrations, such as the fire that destroyed Grenfell Tower in London in 2017. People drown in horrendous tsunamis, such as the one that overwhelmed parts of Asia in 2004. The effect of Covid-19 is still being felt now. The promise in Isaiah does not offer immunity against death, but rather transcendence.

The divine promise is this: if you desire to become fully the person God is dreaming you to be, then follow the way that Jesus walks, learning from him what this fullness of life looks like in human form. This way will inevitably lead to the threshold of death, and here too Jesus says: stay close to me and trust me, for I walk with you every step of the way, and together we will transcend death and embrace the eternal life that we call resurrection.

---

*God does not take the cup of death away from us
but drinks its bitter contents with us, to the very last drop.*

MARGARET SILF

Fountain of life

For he will deliver you from the snare of the fowler and from the deadly pestilence; he will cover you with his pinions, and under his wings you will find refuge; his faithfulness is a shield and buckler. You will not fear the terror of the night, or the arrow that flies by day, or the pestilence that stalks in darkness, or the destruction that wastes at noonday. A thousand may fall at your side, ten thousand at your right hand, but it will not come near you.

In 1845 the town of Dresden in Saxony, Germany, came through a cholera epidemic. In thanksgiving a stone water fountain was erected in the centre of the city, with part of today's reading engraved on it. It was known as the Cholera Fountain, and everyone who used it was reminded of how the city had been saved from 'the pestilence that stalks in darkness'.

In February 1945 Dresden, which was full of refugees, was carpet-bombed by the British overnight, while American snipers picked off any survivors the following day. The city and thousands of its inhabitants were destroyed in the attack, which has since been widely acknowledged as a war crime. The Cholera Fountain, however, survived the bombing raids; it survived 'the terror of the night' and 'the arrow that flies by day', leaving only 'the destruction that wastes at noonday'. It was almost the only construction left standing, its water still faithfully flowing.

Since I first saw it, the Cholera Fountain has been for me a symbol of how the love and faithfulness of God, the source of living water, survive and transcend what seems to be total destruction. It reminds me that the power of love is always stronger than the power of death.

There is a terrible irony now in the words engraved on that fountain, in the face of the city's destruction, but there is also an all-powerful truth: life will always ultimately prevail over death. Our physical life is mortal, and can be destroyed in a heartbeat, but the spring of eternal life can never be extinguished. The source of life and love never ceases to flow.

When we taste the cup of death, may it become for us
the spring of eternal life.

MARGARET SILF

Can these dead bones live?

The hand of the Lord came upon me... and set me down in the middle of a valley; it was full of bones... He said to me, 'Mortal, can these bones live?' I answered, 'O Lord God, you know.' Then he said to me, 'Prophesy to these bones, and say to them... I will cause breath to enter you, and you shall live. I will lay sinews on you, and will cause flesh to come upon you, and cover you with skin, and put breath in you, and you shall live.'

A colleague came to work one morning in a very distressed state. His wife, who was pregnant with their first child, had just been diagnosed with an aggressive form of cancer. She needed treatment urgently if her life was to be saved, but that treatment would kill the unborn child. They were in the depths of despair as they faced this deadly dilemma.

A few weeks passed. They delayed her treatment until, they hoped, their baby might be viable. She shrank down to skin and bones, only the baby bump proclaiming that her dying body contained life. He watched her disappearing before his eyes, even as he watched the new life claim her space. How could these dead bones live?

Then one day he came to the office, and for the first time there was just the hint of a spring in his step. He managed a weak smile, as he told me about the fuchsia bush in their garden. 'It depressed us so much,' he confessed. 'It just died away when winter came, and we knew she would die too. But today we saw the signs of new shoots – as though its death had been just a deep winter sleep.' Fuchsias do that, he realised. But this one was surely a message from God.

Whatever happened to their little family, he knew now that death would never be a permanent reality, but would be more like the winter sleep of a beautiful fuchsia bush. It gave him the courage to carry on, and the faith to keep believing in life, even when life seemed to be totally extinct.

May the breath of the Spirit enter us, that even as we die, yet we shall live.

MARGARET SILF

Out of the depths

Out of the depths I cry to you, O Lord. Lord, hear my voice! Let your ears be attentive to the voice of my supplications… I wait for the Lord, my soul waits, and in his word I hope; my soul waits for the Lord more than those who watch for the morning, more than those who watch for the morning. O Israel, hope in the Lord! For with the Lord there is steadfast love.

Today's reading surely speaks to the heart of anyone who has kept vigil at the bedside of a dying loved one. For me it recalls powerfully the last weeks of my mother's life. I remember my desperate, conflicted prayers as she battled on from one agonising day to the next – prayers that alternated between 'Please, Lord, just give us another day' and 'Take her, Lord, and end her anguish.'

During those weeks I spent many a long night at her bedside, helplessly watching her restless struggle with pain and fear. Then, each night, she would finally find some level of fitful sleep, just before the dawn. While she slept I would slip outside into the garden of my childhood home. It was summertime and dawn came early. The morning chorus greeted me and the scent of the wild roses calmed my troubled heart. Those were blessed times, right in the heart of the torment. The presence of grace was palpable there in those early mornings. Each tortured night I had longed for the morning, and every morning the dawnlight dispelled the night's shadows.

She died at dawn. She entered her new life accompanied not by angel harps but by the song of the garden birds, chorusing their joy that another dawn had broken. I walked one last time through the garden I had loved. Children were playing in a neighbour's garden, and I consciously passed on to them the legacy of my own childhood in that place. Then with a heart heavy with grief yet light with gratitude, I said my last farewell to the one who had given me life.

Words cannot express the depth of our longing for the dawn in a world racked with suffering. And the longed-for morning never, ever fails to respond to our hearts' calls.

MARGARET SILF

God in the stony place

[Jacob] came to a certain place and stayed there for the night, because the sun had set. Taking one of the stones of the place, he put it under his head and lay down in that place. And he dreamed that there was a ladder set up on the earth, the top of it reaching to heaven; and the angels of God were ascending and descending on it… Then Jacob woke from his sleep and said, 'Surely the Lord is in this place – and I did not know it!'

It has been wisely remarked that growing old is not for the faint-hearted. Many of us discover the truth of this observation as one by one our faculties begin to fail, and the things we used to do so easily now cost us more and more effort and energy. It can feel like death by a thousand diminishments.

A friend had been going through a series of painful life events that had left her with mobility impairment and a series of other health issues and was generously supported by several kind friends and neighbours, who were helping her in any ways they could. One day she was attending a scripture study circle and the group was reflecting together on today's reading about Jacob's famous ladder. She was very thoughtful throughout the meeting, and, shortly before the end of the gathering, she shared this insight: 'I have read this passage so often,' she said, 'but until today I had never realised that it's not just about Jacob, but about me. I know that lonely place where Jacob spent the night. I know the stony ground and the hard pillow. But I also know those angels moving up and down the ladder to support me. It's the story of the last few years of my life. But today I've come to recognise that however stony the road may be, the Lord is in this place and I never knew it, until now.'

Perhaps your own road is a stony one. Could it also be the place on earth where the ladder that connects you to heaven begins?

Take time today to notice the human angels on your own 'Jacob's ladder',
bringing you evidence of God's unfailing love for you.

MARGARET SILF

Nothing wasted

As the heavens are higher than the earth, so are my ways higher than your ways and my thoughts than your thoughts. For as the rain and the snow come down from heaven, and do not return there until they have watered the earth, making it bring forth and sprout, giving seed to the sower and bread to the eater, so shall my word be that goes out from my mouth; it shall not return to me empty, but it shall accomplish that which I purpose and succeed in the thing for which I sent it.

A good friend, approaching the last few weeks of his life, was plagued by the question: 'Has my time on earth amounted to anything worthwhile?' In fact, thousands of people had been inspired, encouraged and guided by his life and work, yet all these fruits, so obvious to those who knew him, seemed totally invisible to him. It reminded me of the little seed that falls into the ground and can have absolutely no idea of the wealth of new life that will arise from that dying.

Today's reading reminds us that, however useless we may feel, especially in the face of imminent death, we are like the 'word' that does not return to God without accomplishing that for which it was sent. The raindrops and snowflakes have no sense of the life they bring to the dry earth or what that watered earth will bring forth, yet each one of them is indispensable to life. How could it be otherwise for us, as we face our ending?

As I write this, there is a recruitment drive for teachers running in the UK, which carries the slogan 'Every lesson shapes a life.' As a teacher labours over marking and lesson-planning, it probably doesn't feel like this. Yet most people can recall how a teacher, or other person involved in their formative years, helped the seeds of their gifts to sprout and grow, perhaps through an encouraging word or patient guiding. In God's economy, nothing is ever wasted. Everything fulfils its purpose.

God won't ask to see our exam certificates. God will count the blessings our lives have bestowed on others, often without our ever realising this was happening.

MARGARET SILF

Emptied out

'Very truly, I tell you, you will weep and mourn, but the world will rejoice; you will have pain, but your pain will turn into joy. When a woman is in labour, she has pain, because her hour has come. But when her child is born, she no longer remembers the anguish because of the joy of having brought a human being into the world. So you have pain now; but I will see you again, and your hearts will rejoice, and no one will take your joy from you.'

A dear friend was dying of colon cancer. He saw dying as a sacred process, with which he wanted to fully and consciously engage, and we watched as he steadily let go, shrinking outwardly as the disease took hold, yet growing spiritually in ways that left us in awe.

Each week Donald, his wife and I shared a little Communion service in their home. He would look back over the week, giving thanks for all the blessings he had received and honestly acknowledging anything he regretted. Led by his example, we tried to do the same. It became a sacred sharing circle.

Then one morning, not long before his passing, we were sitting together as usual. His wife had lit the candle and I was reading the day's gospel. Suddenly the candle flame flickered and went out. It felt as though a cold shadow had passed over us. We all knew that what had happened to the candle would happen to Donald soon, and we were close to tears.

But then Donald himself reached out, tipped up the candle, pouring out the excess molten wax, and the flame leapt to life again, as suddenly as it had died. Our hearts leapt for joy, too, because what had happened to the candle would also happen to Donald.

It wasn't a miracle. Candles behave like that when they are drowning in their own wax and need to be emptied out. Yet it was a miracle, because in just a moment it turned our pain into joy. It was a God-given foretaste of a promise in the process of being fulfilled, a life in the process of moving beyond death.

Death's emptying out makes space for eternal life to fill us.

MARGARET SILF

When words fail

And I heard a loud voice from the throne saying, 'See, the home of God is among mortals. He will dwell with them; they will be his peoples, and God himself will be with them; he will wipe every tear from their eyes. Death will be no more; mourning and crying and pain will be no more, for the first things have passed away.' And the one who was seated on the throne said, 'See, I am making all things new.'

Every death is hard on those who are left behind, but perhaps the most devastating of all is the loss of a child. It was to such an event that a very inexperienced young priest was called one day, in response to a heart-rending appeal from the child's mother. When he arrived at the home of the bereaved family, the father was visibly displeased to see a cleric on the doorstep. 'Your wife called me,' the priest explained. 'Well, you'd better not come here with any of the stuff about God wanting another little angel,' the father growled as he reluctantly let him in.

Surrounded by the grieving family, the priest felt utterly helpless. He had no words, no wisdom to offer that might have been remotely adequate, but, overcome himself by the sorrow at the loss of this child, all he could do was stand and weep.

A few weeks passed. One day the bereaved father happened to meet the priest in town. To the priest's surprise, he approached him, holding out his hand. 'I want to thank you,' he said. 'If you had come to us that day with any religious platitudes, I think I might have hit you. But you simply stood alongside us and wept with us. Thank you… for your tears.'

Today's reading promises that every tear shall be wiped away, but before tears can be wiped away they must first be shed. God suffers and weeps with us, before God can wipe away our tears, and he asks us to do the same for each other. When words fail, tears can fall, and the slow journey to healing can begin.

*The light of God's love shining through the tears of our grief
has the power to make all things new.*

MARGARET SILF

Separation

Who will separate us from the love of Christ? Will hardship, or distress, or persecution, or famine, or nakedness, or peril, or sword? As it is written, 'For your sake we are being killed all day long; we are accounted as sheep to be slaughtered.' No, in all these things we are more than conquerors through him who loved us. For I am convinced that neither death, nor life, nor angels, nor rulers, nor things present, nor things to come, nor powers, nor height, nor depth, nor anything else in all creation, will be able to separate us from the love of God in Christ Jesus our Lord.

None of us likes to be separated, even temporarily, from those we love or from what is familiar to us, and we can imagine no greater, more final separation than death. Death parts us from loved ones, perhaps from lifelong partners and friends, and ruthlessly strips us of all that is familiar. Death closes down all we have known and loved and opens up a chasm of unknowing, flooding us with apprehension. How might today's reading offer us authentic reassurance?

When I think of the threat of separation, I imagine a great wheel with an infinite number of spokes radiating out from a central hub. If I think of myself as one of those spokes, gazing out into the emptiness of space, I can easily feel alone and separated from the other spokes, with no obvious connection to the wheel. But if I focus back towards the hub, I realise that I belong to something much greater than myself, placed there securely and for all time and eternity by the divine wheelwright.

The fear of separation is real, and no easy clichés will dismiss it. Almost all infants experience separation anxiety when parted from their parents or caregivers, until they realise that people do not cease to exist just because you cannot see them. Is this not also true for us? Do we truly trust that those we love do not cease to exist just because we can no longer see them?

Death does not remove the beloved from the wheel of life;
it merely extends the range of that life beyond the horizon of
human vision and understanding.

MARGARET SILF

Depart in peace

It had been revealed to [Simeon] by the Holy Spirit that he would not see death before he had seen the Lord's Messiah. Guided by the Spirit, Simeon came into the temple; and when the parents brought in the child Jesus, to do for him what was customary under the law, Simeon took him in his arms and praised God, saying, 'Master, now you are dismissing your servant in peace, according to your word; for my eyes have seen your salvation, which you have prepared in the presence of all peoples.'

These beautiful words, spoken by an old man in the temple as he holds the newborn Jesus in his arms, are perhaps among the best loved in all of scripture, repeated as they are every time we pray the Nunc Dimittis.

Simeon is standing at journey's end, cradling the infant Jesus right at the beginning of his earthly journey. What a poignant moment, not just for Simeon but for Mary and Joseph too. It echoes and prefigures millions of similar moments when an ageing friend or relative takes a new arrival in their arms. The tears of joy that flow in such moments are surely their own kind of baptism.

In this sacred human ritual the very old welcomes the brand new; an imminent ending welcomes a new beginning; the tangled script of experience welcomes the blank slate of future possibility. God is making all things new. Had we been present at this encounter, we would surely have taken off our shoes, because this is holy ground.

The ground is no less holy when we are the ones who stand at death's door. Simeon is all our grandfathers, inviting us to acknowledge those moments when we too have known, with personal heart-knowledge, the reality of God's love and presence.

We have all known such moments, each in our own way. Guided by the Spirit, we can all say, with Simeon, 'With my own eyes, and in my own life, I have seen your salvation.' May we also be able, when the time is right, to pray with Simeon, 'Now, Lord, let your servant depart in peace.'

May Simeon's prayer assure us that our death is not a fracturing but a completion of the circle of life.

MARGARET SILF

The character of a saint

When I pondered what forms the character of a saint, I thought of Hebrews 11. It is one of my favourite passages in scripture, with its inspiring Hall of Faith – those from the Old Testament who served God faithfully, believing in his promises while welcoming them at a distance. They trusted in God and acted on their beliefs through faith.

But as I dug into the individual stories of these saints, I was reminded of their foibles. Although the writer to the Hebrews doesn't name any of their failings, their stories in the Old Testament make clear their sins and errors. In short, they are a motley bunch. They are liars, those overcome with fear, a murderer, a deceiver; they make errors in judgement and fall into sin. But in the Hebrews account, they are commended for their acts of faith. God used them in spite of their failings and sins, which I find greatly encouraging.

Our list of saints includes those about whom we know little, such as Abel and Enoch, along with those about whom we know much more. Abraham and Sarah feature prominently as those who left their home country, becoming foreigners and strangers in a land God led them to, set aside for his people. The story of Abraham's line continues with Isaac, Jacob and Joseph, with themes of favouritism, betrayal and heartache, along with the exercise of faith. The list includes some who might surprise us, such as Rahab, a prostitute who lied, and Samson, a brutal man who didn't honour God fully.

We examine their lives during the middle of the season of Lent. Perhaps it feels like the 'messy middle' of this season – we've passed the first rush of inspiration and the end isn't yet in sight. As we read about the lives of others – the good, the bad and the ugly – we can consider how to build our own character during the messy middle of various seasons we experience.

Saints, whatever their failings, are those who long for 'a better country – a heavenly one' (Hebrews 11:16, NIV). God commended them for their faith; what's remembered is not their sins but the ways they believed and trusted in God. May that be true of us too.

AMY BOUCHER PYE

Faith in action: Abel

Now faith is confidence in what we hope for and assurance about what we do not see. This is what the ancients were commended for. By faith we understand that the universe was formed at God's command, so that what is seen was not made out of what was visible. By faith Abel brought God a better offering than Cain did. By faith he was commended as righteous, when God spoke well of his offerings. And by faith Abel still speaks, even though he is dead.

Abel might not be the first person who comes to mind when we think of Old Testament saints, but he's the first person the writer to the Hebrews lists as those commended for their faith. We read his story in Genesis 4, where he and his brother Cain, the sons of the first parents, give their offerings to God. Abel offers to God some of the fat of the firstborn of his flock, but Cain brings only some fruits of the soil. God receives Abel's offering but not Cain's, and in a premeditated jealous rage, the older brother kills the younger. We could therefore view Abel as the first martyr – he died doing what was right before God, killed by one who did not.

We don't know much about Abel, but his offering in the Genesis account speaks for him. Knowing what God required, he gave faithfully from the best of his flock, not holding back. He honoured God, his actions reflecting the state of his heart.

On that day Abel may have gone about his sacrifice with an attitude of normality, not guessing that this would be one of the last things he did, nor that he would be remembered all these years later as one who is righteous. He lived as an ordinary saint. We too can offer our best efforts to God, serving him quietly and faithfully, knowing that he sees us and receives our offerings.

'With this in mind, we constantly pray for you, that our God may make you worthy of his calling, and that by his power he may bring to fruition your every desire for goodness and your every deed prompted by faith' (2 Thessalonians 1:11).

AMY BOUCHER PYE

Walking with God: Enoch and Noah

By faith Enoch was taken from this life, so that he did not experience death: 'He could not be found, because God had taken him away.' For before he was taken, he was commended as one who pleased God. And without faith it is impossible to please God, because anyone who comes to him must believe that he exists and that he rewards those who earnestly seek him. By faith Noah, when warned about things not yet seen, in holy fear built an ark to save his family. By his faith he condemned the world and became heir of the righteousness that is in keeping with faith.

In this list of faith-filled heroes, the writer to the Hebrews names another ordinary saint, Enoch, about whom we know little. Genesis 5:24 says that he 'walked faithfully with God' – his day-to-day life pleased the Lord. What's a bit unusual about him is that he is one of the two people named in the Bible who didn't experience death but were taken by God to heaven (Elijah being the other).

As we aren't told why he didn't die in the normal way, and why he received this special treatment, perhaps it's best to focus on what we do know – his faithful walking with God. Walking implies a journey of intent. Through the ordinary placing of one step in front of the other we travel either towards right living or away from it. Our actions reveal our inner motives.

The writer also names Noah in this list, and we know much more about him, for he obeyed God by building the ark. He too is named as one who is righteous, for his faith led him to follow God as he endured ridicule from onlookers. Again the writer to the Hebrews centres on actions as key to the lives of the saints. What we do – how we follow God through our daily walk in our homes, work and communities – reveals the state of our hearts towards God.

What will you do today?

Lord God, you call me to follow you through the mundane acts I will do today. Help me to live for you with faith and hope.

AMY BOUCHER PYE

Faith through foibles: Abraham

By faith Abraham, when called to go to a place he would later receive as his inheritance, obeyed and went, even though he did not know where he was going. By faith he made his home in the promised land like a stranger in a foreign country... For he was looking forward to the city with foundations, whose architect and builder is God... By faith Abraham, when God tested him, offered Isaac as a sacrifice. He who had embraced the promises was about to sacrifice his one and only son... Abraham reasoned that God could even raise the dead, and so in a manner of speaking he did receive Isaac back from death.

In our list of Old Testament saints, we reach one, Abraham, whom the Bible describes in great detail. Whereas we could be tempted to memorialise Abel and Enoch because of their sparse biographies, we see Abraham with his failures and foibles – and his great faith. For instance, as Genesis 12 recounts, when in Egypt, Abraham passed his wife Sarah off as his sister, in effect trafficking her to Pharaoh. Thankfully the Lord intervened, sending diseases on Pharaoh's house, so Sarah was returned to her husband. Abraham was not without stain, but as he learned to trust God he became the father of many.

He exercised faith, following God's call as he left his earthly riches and became a nomad, one who lived in tents without knowing what the final destination would be. He and Sarah believed that God would give them a son, and they waited for decades for the fulfilment of that promise. Then after all of the longing and hoping, Abraham showed how strong his trust in God had become, for he was willing to sacrifice Isaac. He believed that God could resurrect Isaac.

Whatever failures we've experienced or foibles we may despair of, we can trust that as we follow God day by day, we'll continue to grow in faith. As God changed Abraham, so will he transform us, making us more like himself.

'What does Scripture say? "Abraham believed God, and it was credited to him as righteousness"' (Romans 4:3).

AMY BOUCHER PYE

Living by faith: Sarah

And by faith even Sarah, who was past childbearing age, was enabled to bear children because she considered him faithful who had made the promise. And so from this one man, and he as good as dead, came descendants as numerous as the stars in the sky and as countless as the sand on the seashore. All these people were still living by faith when they died. They did not receive the things promised; they only saw them and welcomed them from a distance, admitting that they were foreigners and strangers on earth… God is not ashamed to be called their God, for he has prepared a city for them.

In *The Meaning Is in the Waiting*, Paula Gooder shares how God's changing of Sarai's name to Sarah reflects his redemptive purposes. Whereas both words mean 'princess' in Hebrew, Sarai sounds like a word that means 'my distress', while Sarah simply evokes the meaning of princess. Thus Sarah, who experienced so much pain in her long wait for God to fulfil his promises, is not remembered for her distress but through her status as one precious to God.

What we read in Hebrews reflects this reality. The passage doesn't mention how Sarah got tired of waiting for the promised heir and so arranged for a surrogacy through her slave, Hagar (see Genesis 16). When Hagar turned on her, Sarah banished Hagar to the desert to die. But God saw Hagar and saved her; he then repeated his promises to Abraham and Sarah to make them a great nation as he invited them to believe him.

The writer to the Hebrews focuses not on the wrongdoing, but on the faith that emerged through the trials. Sarah and Abraham didn't experience all of the promises as fulfilled right away; they welcomed them from a distance. They believed that God would follow through – in this world and in the next.

As you consider any trials you're experiencing, think back to other testing times and ask God to reveal how he was with you in the midst of them.

Father God, thank you for seeing us as those created in your image and likeness. Forgive me for doubting you. Build my faith that I might believe.

AMY BOUCHER PYE

Faith for the future: Isaac

So Isaac called for Jacob and blessed him. Then he commanded him: 'Do not marry a Canaanite woman. Go at once to Paddan Aram, to the house of your mother's father Bethuel. Take a wife for yourself there, from among the daughters of Laban, your mother's brother. May God Almighty bless you and make you fruitful and increase your numbers until you become a community of peoples. May he give you and your descendants the blessing given to Abraham, so that you may take possession of the land where you now reside as a foreigner, the land God gave to Abraham.'

Isaac, spared from being sacrificed by his father, served God faithfully throughout his life. Even so, he wasn't perfect – he followed his father's actions in passing off his wife Rebekah as his sister when he felt threatened by the Philistines, and he favoured his elder son Esau over the younger Jacob. This preferential treatment of his sons set them against each other, especially because Rebekah favoured Jacob.

Yet Isaac is named as one of the Old Testament people of faith by the writer to the Hebrews. He is acclaimed for blessing his sons regarding their futures by faith (Hebrews 11:20). Although he set them at odds against each other, he trusted God for how their lives would turn out and how God would keep the promises he made to his father, Abraham. How this happened was complicated – Jacob tricked Isaac into giving him the blessing he intended for Esau. After bestowing this blessing on Jacob, Isaac could only bless Esau with a lesser blessing; then Isaac blessed Jacob again, passing along the covenantal blessing. Because of this final blessing, Jacob became the father of the twelve tribes of Israel.

From Isaac we learn that the character of a saint entails keeping faith in God, even when we face a messy situation that we in part created. We can't control the future, but we can trust that God will keep his promises and stay by our side.

Lord, I know I can make a mess of things, including my relationships. Please help me to sort out what's in a tangle as I trust you for my future.

AMY BOUCHER PYE

A changed man: Jacob

When Israel saw the sons of Joseph, he asked, 'Who are these?' 'They are the sons God has given me here,' Joseph said to his father. Then Israel said… 'May the God before whom my fathers Abraham and Isaac walked faithfully… bless these boys… May they increase greatly on the earth'… Joseph… took hold of his father's hand to move it from Ephraim's head to Manasseh's head… But his father refused and said, 'I know, my son, I know. He too will become a people, and he too will become great. Nevertheless, his younger brother will be greater than he, and his descendants will become a group of nations.'

A man named Jacob, which means 'deceiver', is yet a hero of the faith, according to Hebrews: 'By faith Jacob, when he was dying, blessed each of Joseph's sons' (Hebrews 11:21). The writer calls him by the name Jacob, even though God changed his name to Israel, which means 'one who struggled with God', after the night-time tussle when he demanded a blessing. He was a changed man, not only in name, but in the limp that reminded him of his meeting with God.

Jacob, like his father, had favourites among his offspring, preferring Joseph and Benjamin, the sons of his beloved wife Rachel. And because of this favouritism he suffered the pain of separation from one of his sons, just like his father had before him, when Joseph was sold as a slave into Egypt. But even as Jacob made amends with the brother whom he had crossed, so did Joseph reach out to his brothers in a wonderful family reunion. Jacob once again had the joy of knowing Joseph. And when Jacob blessed his grandsons on his deathbed, he bypassed tradition and gave the blessing of the elder to the younger – just as he himself had received Esau's blessing.

Jacob didn't live as a deceiver all of his life, but became the father of the nation of Israel. He died in faith, knowing that God would continue to dwell with his people.

Father of Abraham, Isaac and Jacob, you've loved your people for generations. Continue to shower your love and mercy on us.

AMY BOUCHER PYE

Faith and forgiveness: Joseph

When Joseph's brothers saw that their father was dead, they said, 'What if Joseph holds a grudge against us and pays us back for all the wrongs we did to him?' So they sent word to Joseph, saying, '… Now please forgive the sins of the servants of the God of your father.' When their message came to him, Joseph wept… Joseph said to them, 'Don't be afraid. Am I in the place of God? You intended to harm me, but God intended it for good to accomplish what is now being done, the saving of many lives. So then, don't be afraid. I will provide for you and your children.' And he reassured them and spoke kindly to them.

Joseph was a man who lived by faith, as Hebrews 11:22 attests: 'By faith Joseph, when his end was near, spoke about the exodus of the Israelites from Egypt.' As we saw yesterday, the fact that he was a favourite of his father changed his life when, at 17, he became a slave in Egypt. There he faced further injustice when the wife of the master he had served faithfully put the moves on him and he was banished to prison. Nevertheless he kept his integrity, and his charisma and God-given ability to interpret dreams led to him eventually being elevated to become Pharaoh's deputy. The timing was God-ordained, for he was able to save his people from starvation when a long drought hit the country.

Perhaps one of the most moving episodes in the biblical narrative comes after Jacob dies, when Joseph's brothers fear for their lives because of the way they had treated him. They ask for his forgiveness, but Joseph responds by pointing to God's purposes and how their earlier transgressions led to him being in the right place at the right time. He looked to God to forgive them.

When we have a choice about forgiving someone – perhaps, like Joseph, a sibling – we too can follow Joseph's example and ask God to help us forgive.

Forgiving Father, you wash me clean of my wrongdoing.
Help me to extend forgiveness and grace to those who wrong me.

AMY BOUCHER PYE

A clean slate: Moses

By faith Moses, when he had grown up, refused to be known as the son of Pharaoh's daughter. He chose to be ill-treated along with the people of God… He regarded disgrace for the sake of Christ as of greater value than the treasures of Egypt, because he was looking ahead to his reward. By faith he left Egypt, not fearing the king's anger; he persevered because he saw him who is invisible. By faith he kept the Passover and the application of blood, so that the destroyer of the firstborn would not touch the firstborn of Israel. By faith the people passed through the Red Sea as on dry land; but when the Egyptians tried to do so, they were drowned.

The writer to the Hebrews shows us what God's forgiveness looks like through their great list of faith-filled heroes. As we ponder these short biographies, we can see slates that have been wiped clean. Take Moses, for example. The words in Hebrews include line after line of the ways Moses followed God – how he relinquished the social standing of being related to Pharaoh, instead siding with God's people; how he left Egypt, persevering through the series of plagues as he led the people into the promised land, exercising faith in God.

Note especially what's not included. One example is his stammer, because of which he asked God to relieve him of the burden of speaking on God's behalf, with the result that his brother Aaron had to be his mouthpiece. Or, notably, Moses' murder of the Egyptian when he witnessed the man beating a fellow Hebrew, after which Moses fled the country for 40 years. On these and other failings, the writer to the Hebrews remains silent.

What would your biography look like? If you have a few moments, try prayerfully writing it as if you were included in Hebrews 11. Note the deeds and actions that would stand out as the things you did 'by faith'. If you were to embrace this point of view in your life today, how might you live differently?

Lord, give me an eternal perspective, that I might see what really matters to you. Help me to live with faith, that I might serve you and share your love.

AMY BOUCHER PYE

No perfect people: Rahab

[Rahab] said to them, 'I know that the Lord has given this land to you and that a great fear of you has fallen on us, so that all who live in this country are melting in fear because of you… Our hearts sank and everyone's courage failed because of you, for the Lord your God is God in heaven above and on the earth below. Now then, please swear to me by the Lord that you will show kindness to my family, because I have shown kindness to you… and that you will save us from death.' 'Our lives for your lives!' the men assured her. 'If you don't tell what we are doing, we will treat you kindly and faithfully when the Lord gives us the land.'

That the writer to the Hebrews mentions two women (Sarah and Rahab) in their list of heroes of the faith would have been countercultural in the ancient world. Rahab (Hebrews 11:31) would not have been seen as a paragon of virtue, for she was a prostitute. And the act that got her mentioned in this list was lying – she lied to the king of Jericho to protect the spies whom Joshua had sent to the promised land.

Rahab had discerned that God was with these men – note how she repeatedly describes the fear that had fallen on her and the other Canaanites because of the Israelites, including the wonderfully visual phrase 'melting in fear'. Acknowledging the power of God, she negotiated safety for herself and her family.

Rahab is listed not only in Hebrews 11 but also in Matthew 1, the genealogy of Jesus. That a so-called fallen woman, who lied and who belonged to a nation opposed to God's people, was yet a hero of the faith and an ancestor of Jesus shows that God doesn't have any perfect people in his tribe. We've seen this theme time and time again in Hebrews 11.

What's the character of a saint? One who believes, even though at times they've failed.

Compassionate one, today we pray for all those who are caught in the sex trade. Release the prisoners; set them free.

AMY BOUCHER PYE

Miracles and torture

I do not have time to tell about Gideon, Barak, Samson and Jephthah, about David and Samuel and the prophets, who through faith conquered kingdoms, administered justice, and gained what was promised; who shut the mouths of lions… whose weakness was turned to strength… Women received back their dead, raised to life again. There were others who were tortured, refusing to be released so that they might gain an even better resurrection. Some faced jeers and flogging, and even chains and imprisonment. They were put to death by stoning; they were sawn in two… They went about in sheepskins and goatskins, destitute, persecuted and ill-treated – the world was not worthy of them.

As we come to the end of the writer's list, they seem to run out of scroll as they grapple with the task of naming all of God's faithful people. So instead they give a summary, naming some heroes whom we will explore for the rest of the week along with this list of amazing deeds. Note that the writer doesn't put the six men in chronological order; rather, they allude to a sample of faithful heroes and don't give an exhaustive record.

The deeds noted here would have brought to mind some of the Old Testament characters – Daniel, who shut the mouths of lions, and Isaiah, who according to legend was sawn in two. This nasty death affirms that living by faith doesn't mean that saints are protected from bad things in this world. They remain faithful to God even though they suffer, are persecuted and often are harmed physically. They follow God at a cost, believing that God will be faithful.

We can ask God to strengthen our faith while pondering not only the miracles that come through the faithful but also their willingness to suffer and not give up. God can work through us so that we can accomplish more than we could ever imagine. And he can help us to keep on keeping on when we feel that we've reached the end of our strength.

Lord Jesus Christ, you experienced the fullness of the human experience, being persecuted and suffering, yet you never gave up. Be with me today.

AMY BOUCHER PYE

From doubt to belief: Gideon

During that night the Lord said to Gideon, 'Get up, go down against the camp, because I am going to give it into your hands. If you are afraid to attack, go down to the camp with your servant Purah and listen to what they are saying. Afterwards, you will be encouraged to attack the camp.' So he and Purah his servant went down to the outposts of the camp… Gideon arrived just as a man was telling a friend his dream… When Gideon heard the dream and its interpretation, he bowed down and worshipped. He returned to the camp of Israel and called out, 'Get up! The Lord has given the Midianite camp into your hands.'

I'm glad that Gideon makes the list in Hebrews 11, for I'm guessing that many of us can relate to him. He didn't feel that he came from a prestigious tribe, nor was he important within that tribe. We meet him in Judges 6, when he is hiding from the Midianites who were thrashing God's people, destroying their crops and taking away their livelihoods. When an angel appeared to him and called him a mighty warrior, he was rather startled, for he didn't think of himself as one.

His story is well known: he questions God three times, doubting the promises God makes to him. The Lord doesn't lose patience with this not-yet-mighty warrior, each time answering his requests. God follows through, and Gideon finally believes. It's only when he overhears the enemy talking about him that he is convinced that he and his pared-down company will triumph. From then on, he leads as a mighty warrior. They save the Israelites and declare victory over their enemies.

At times we all face fear of various kinds. But as we look to God for his help, we find comfort and strength. We don't have to feel strong to do the next right thing or act on the nudge we sense from the Holy Spirit. As we press forward step by step, we'll grow in courage, knowing that God is with us.

Loving Lord, thank you for your patience when I question and doubt you.
I believe; help my unbelief.

AMY BOUCHER PYE

God's ways: Samson

Now the rulers of the Philistines assembled to offer a great sacrifice to Dagon their god and to celebrate, saying, 'Our god has delivered Samson, our enemy, into our hands'… While they were in high spirits, they shouted, 'Bring out Samson to entertain us'… Now the temple was crowded with men and women; all the rulers of the Philistines were there, and on the roof were about three thousand men and women… Then Samson prayed to the Lord, 'Sovereign Lord, remember me. Please, God, strengthen me just once more, and let me with one blow get revenge on the Philistines for my two eyes'… Samson said, 'Let me die with the Philistines!' Then he pushed with all his might, and down came the temple on the rulers and all the people in it.

I'm guessing that we'll find it harder to relate to Samson than we did to Gideon yesterday, for Samson acted impulsively and brutally. He had been a gift to his infertile parents and was set aside from birth as a Nazirite, one who was not to drink alcohol or cut his hair. Indeed, the secret to his massive strength lay in his hair – if it was cut, his strength would seep away from him.

Throughout his life he killed many, sometimes seemingly randomly, such as those who couldn't guess the answer to a riddle that he had posed. But his weakness was women. Delilah would lead to his downfall, needling him day after day to reveal the secret to his strength. He finally gave in, she cut his hair and he lost his sight and was imprisoned. But God heard his last plea for help against the Philistines, enabling him to bring destruction on them and himself.

Samson seems a selfish man who focused on his own agenda. We don't know why God consecrated him for special service, why he didn't turn God's people back to worshipping God or even why he was included in Hebrews 11. Perhaps his inclusion is a reminder that God's ways are his own and that we don't always understand them.

Lord, bring us wisdom and understanding and the grace to know our limitations. Work through us to share your love and peace.

AMY BOUCHER PYE

One after God's own heart: David

When they arrived, Samuel saw Eliab and thought, 'Surely the Lord's anointed stands here before the Lord.' But the Lord said to Samuel, 'Do not consider his appearance or his height, for I have rejected him. The Lord does not look at the things people look at. People look at the outward appearance, but the Lord looks at the heart'... So he asked Jesse, 'Are these all the sons you have?' 'There is still the youngest,' Jesse answered. 'He is tending the sheep'... Then the Lord said, 'Rise and anoint him; this is the one.' So Samuel took the horn of oil and anointed him in the presence of his brothers, and from that day on the Spirit of the Lord came powerfully upon David.

If we were to put together a Hall of Faith such as the one in Hebrews 11, I'm guessing that David might be one of the first we'd include. Twice in the Bible he's called a man after God's own heart (1 Samuel 13:14; Acts 13:22); he's one who followed God with passion and commitment – mostly. He is the character who appears the most in the Old Testament, in 66 chapters, and he is referred to 59 times in the New Testament. He's the unlikely leader, appointed by Samuel, a warrior king who was also a poet and musician.

David only 'mostly' followed God. For example, there was the blip he had one spring, when he stayed back in the palace instead of going off to war with his troops. When his eye was drawn to the beauty of Bathsheba on a nearby roof, he exercised his power as a king for his own pleasure, with tragic results. But after he sinned, he repented fully, penning the glorious song of repentance, Psalm 51.

God chose David as his leader, and David followed him with passion and perseverance through hardship and trials. After he took the sinful detour, he recommitted himself to serving God wholeheartedly, a decision that we too can follow as we seek to be those after God's own heart.

Lord, when I turn from you, have mercy on me and cleanse me from my sins. Teach me your ways, that I might always follow you.

AMY BOUCHER PYE

Commended for his faith: Samuel

The people all said to Samuel, 'Pray to the Lord your God for your servants so that we will not die, for we have added to all our other sins the evil of asking for a king.' 'Do not be afraid,' Samuel replied. 'You have done all this evil; yet do not turn away from the Lord, but serve the Lord with all your heart. Do not turn away after useless idols... For the sake of his great name the Lord will not reject his people, because the Lord was pleased to make you his own. As for me, far be it from me that I should sin against the Lord by failing to pray for you. And I will teach you the way that is good and right.'

Samuel is the last person listed in Hebrews 11 as a person of faith. Perhaps he's listed last because he lived faithfully before God, serving him without a major failing. He was a Nazirite, like Samson, but unlike the strongman he fulfilled the special call on his life through his service to God. He was a prophet and a priest; he was the last judge of Israel and the one who anointed their first two kings, Saul and David. But he knew that God's people could easily idolise their earthly king and forget the living God, so he counselled them against this move. Yet when they insisted, he didn't give up on them. He kept on praying for them and directing them back to God. When he saw King Saul going astray, he orchestrated David to be crowned king. It's fitting that he takes the final position in this Hall of Faith.

The character of a saint is one who holds to their faith in God. As the writer to the Hebrews said, 'These were all commended for their faith, yet none of them received what had been promised, since God had planned something better for us so that only together with us would they be made perfect' (Hebrews 11:39–40). May we hold strongly to God, that we too one day will be made perfect.

Father, Son and Holy Spirit, dwell with us
that we might increase our faith in you.

AMY BOUCHER PYE

Lent and Holy Week in John

John's gospel is full of contrasts: night and day, heaven and earth, light and darkness and so on. There is exploration of the nature of God: Father, Son, Spirit. God's relationship with humanity is characterised by light, life and love. Discipleship of Jesus is described in terms of faith, humility, obedience and community. For Christians who, at this time of year, want to examine themselves before God and open themselves to engaging more with God, John's gospel offers riches beyond compare.

Perhaps the most obvious texts in John's gospel in the last week of Lent are Jesus' words and actions in the upper room (chapters 13—16) and Jesus' prayer for his disciples, the church and the world (chapter 17). The subsequent chapters could then be read in Holy Week to remind us of Jesus' arrest, trial and crucifixion as portrayed by John. *New Daylight* notes have done this in the past to excellent effect. Yet for some Christians, Passion Sunday (the Sunday before Palm Sunday) marks a change from examining how we follow Jesus to a focus on Jesus himself.

With this in mind, the first few studies will examine Jesus' encounters with individuals as they move towards (or away from) the light of revelation of who Jesus is and his purpose in the world. The account of Palm Sunday will be followed by reflections on the betrayal of Jesus first by Judas, then Peter, then the crowd. On Maundy Thursday we bask in the exquisite description of Jesus washing his disciples' feet, while Good Friday shows how Jesus loved his own to the end. Finally, Holy Saturday offers the story of Jesus' burial by two disciples, one of whom is Nicodemus, whom we will also encounter in the first study.

As usual, the printed passages offer only a snapshot of Jesus' words and works, and I would urge you to study the set reading in context. In fact, you might want to spend some time before Easter reading through the whole of John's gospel. Discover something new about faith in the God who came to save us and how to live this to God's glory.

In the following notes I draw on Rodney A. Whitacre's commentary on John (IVP, 1999) and conversations with Dr David Wenham, to whom I am indebted.

LAKSHMI JEFFREYS

The ultimate purpose

'No one has ascended into heaven except the one who descended from heaven, the Son of Man. And just as Moses lifted up the serpent in the wilderness, so must the Son of Man be lifted up, that whoever believes in him may have eternal life. For God so loved the world that he gave his only Son, so that everyone who believes in him may not perish but may have eternal life.'

Some years after I was ordained, I met an experienced priest who was at the time, like me, a single woman in a role which did not involve leading a parish church. Her sense of humour was at once dry and zany; she was creative; she was utterly dependent on God while remaining supremely self-possessed. This woman was a fabulous role model for me.

The problem with role models is that they can easily become idols. Rather than looking at Jesus, we look at the individual we admire and seek to emulate them. Perhaps this is what some of the religious teachers did with Moses, claiming that he had ascended into heaven. Jesus refutes this as he asserts that only the Son of Man (himself) has ascended into heaven. Moses lifted up the serpent in the wilderness (thereby bringing healing to God's wayward people who looked at it), while the Son of Man would be lifted up by God on the cross. Moses was doing what God ordered so that those who were dying would live. Jesus was sent by God from heaven: those who looked at him on the cross would have eternal life.

The context of the passage is Jesus' conversation with Nicodemus, who is challenged to believe that Jesus has come from God. Other Pharisees would not approve. They are portrayed in John's gospel as people who value their traditions and the maintenance of the current hierarchy more than the possibility of an encounter with the true Messiah. Nicodemus begins to leave such ideas behind and focus on Jesus himself.

Who are your role models or people who have influenced you positively? Thank God and ask for the ability to see Jesus more clearly through what you admire about them. You and they are among those whom God loves so much that he sent Jesus.

LAKSHMI JEFFREYS

Saviour of the world

Many Samaritans from that city believed in him because of the woman's testimony, 'He told me everything I have ever done.' So when the Samaritans came to him, they asked him to stay with them; and he stayed there for two days. And many more believed because of his word. They said to the woman, 'It is no longer because of what you said that we believe, for we have heard for ourselves, and we know that this is truly the Saviour of the world.'

This passage is the end of the story of a Samaritan woman who had a strong sense that the world was not as it should be, but that one day God would act to put things right. Having demonstrated his knowledge of the truth about the woman's life, Jesus tells her that he is the Messiah. The woman returns to her village and invites others to come with her to see a man who knew everything about her and still accepted her. Could he be the awaited Saviour? Intrigued, the villagers see Jesus for themselves and invite him to stay in their village. As a result, their faith in Jesus moves from being based on the woman's testimony to being based on their own experience of Jesus.

A friend became a committed disciple of Jesus a year or so before we met. She, like the Samaritan woman, continues to have an overwhelming desire to introduce Jesus to everyone she knows. She has an instinct about when to offer to pray with or for people, regardless of their religious belief. As a result, people of various faiths or none ask her to speak to Jesus, initially on their behalf and, over time, alongside them, until they are able to embrace the Christian faith for themselves.

In an age of global religious intolerance and bigotry, alongside fanaticism and desperation to proselytise, there has never been a greater need for the Saviour of the world to be known. Perhaps evangelism with integrity comes when we are so captivated by Jesus that we naturally introduce him to others, trusting God with the consequences.

How does Jesus' encounter with the Samaritan woman challenge you as you consider God's work of salvation, especially relating to people of other faiths?

LAKSHMI JEFFREYS

Suffering and God's glory

His disciples asked him, 'Rabbi, who sinned, this man or his parents, that he was born blind?' Jesus answered, 'Neither this man nor his parents sinned; he was born blind so that God's works might be revealed in him. We must work the works of him who sent me while it is day; night is coming when no one can work. As long as I am in the world, I am the light of the world.'

There remains today, as in Jesus' time, the belief that bad things happen to people who anger God in some way. Of course, some suffering is a direct result of sin, as a friend ruefully acknowledged when fined for speeding. In today's passage, Jesus shows that suffering allows manifestation of God's glory. Jesus declares that he is the light of the world while he is in the world. (Throughout John's gospel, 'night' refers to the time when Jesus is absent.) Sent by God to do God's work, Jesus brings light, both physical and spiritual, as the blind man follows Jesus' instructions and his sight is restored. At the end of the story, it becomes clear that the light of the world leaves some people blind to God's ways and, crucially, to God's Messiah. Perhaps an experience of suffering can bring us closer to God when we trust Jesus.

I was watching a county cricket match; the batsman struck the ball, which bounced and hit me in the face, fracturing my cheek and nose. Despite knowing the injuries were serious, I had a strange sense of thankfulness that no one else had been hurt: I knew that I would be okay, but another person might not have the same understanding. Even in the following days, when I looked like one of the less attractive monsters from *Doctor Who* and the 'what ifs' began, I wasn't angry or bitter. Jesus was with me in a profound manner. While I never want to go through anything like that again, God's blessings were life-changing. I could not have experienced them any other way.

Gracious God, free me from the desire to cling to what I know and thereby become resentful. Instead, please use my suffering to your glory as I find comfort in you (after Whitacre, p. 237).

LAKSHMI JEFFREYS

Abundant life

Jesus said to them, 'Very truly, I tell you, I am the gate for the sheep. All who came before me are thieves and bandits; but the sheep did not listen to them. I am the gate. Whoever enters by me will be saved, and will come in and go out and find pasture. The thief comes only to steal and kill and destroy. I came that they may have life, and have it abundantly.'

During the summer in the Middle East, sheep are sometimes kept in the pasture overnight. Rocks are piled up to make a pen and the shepherd lies across the entrance, becoming the gate for the sheep. Jesus' original hearers would have been familiar with the image and therefore the implications of Jesus protecting those in his care from attack. But there is a twist to the story: Jesus is there not simply to protect the sheep but as the entrance to the pen. In other words, in order to belong to God's people, followers must come and go through Jesus. Doing this, they will find 'pasture', all they need to meet their physical and spiritual requirements. The thief is interested only in his or her own needs and will steal, kill and destroy the sheep. Jesus has been sent by God to bring God's life to all who accept him.

So many people settle for the adequate or insufficient, rather than accepting Jesus' offer of abundance. The atheist, struggling with personal illness and wider difficulties, admitted that he did not want to believe in God, even if the Christian proved God's existence. Unfortunately the same attitude is sometimes found in Christians, who want Jesus to protect them and work on their behalf but do not want Jesus to be in charge. Society tells us we need to be self-reliant and offers numerous ways to live on our terms, striving for what we believe we need and usually being disappointed. Jesus offers us life in God on God's terms.

Nelson Mandela said, 'There is no passion to be found playing small – in settling for a life that is less than the one you are capable of living.' Loving God, forgive my self-reliance and fear and teach me to live fully in you.

LAKSHMI JEFFREYS

Death…

The disciples said to him, 'Lord, if he has fallen asleep, he will be all right.' Jesus, however, had been speaking about his death, but they thought that he was referring merely to sleep. Then Jesus told them plainly, 'Lazarus is dead. For your sake I am glad I was not there, so that you may believe. But let us go to him.' Thomas, who was called the Twin, said to his fellow-disciples, 'Let us also go, that we may die with him.'

While Martha and Mary are found in various gospel accounts, Lazarus, their brother, appears only in chapters 11 and 12 of John's gospel. Jesus' love for this family is never in question, although his actions might apparently suggest otherwise, since he refuses to visit Lazarus until after Lazarus has died. Jesus' disciples have no idea what is happening, appearing extraordinarily dense, suggesting Jesus might undertake a journey into enemy territory simply to be an alarm clock for his friend! Despite misunderstanding the circumstances, Thomas demonstrates astonishing faith: if Jesus sees the need to go, everyone should follow, even if they die together.

Jesus is the way, not merely a signpost, so we travel with him. Faith is required when the destination is uncertain and death might be involved, either the death of hopes or expectations or even literal death. It can be difficult when we do not understand Jesus' actions in particular situations, which appear obvious to us. As someone who supports people exploring ordination in the Church of England, I have the privilege of witnessing the courage of individuals as they discern their next step with the Lord. Sometimes there is a need to make significant personal or financial sacrifices. On other occasions someone might have to rethink everything about God's call, if the outcome is not what was expected. Yet God rewards faithfulness, as one person discovered, laying down a desire they had cherished for years, before taking up the real call on their life.

Thomas is known as 'doubting Thomas', perhaps unfairly, given his willingness to go with Jesus whatever the cost. Unlike Thomas and the others, we know the end of the story. That might help us exercise faith, even in the face of death.

Lord, where you go, may I follow.

LAKSHMI JEFFREYS

... and resurrection

Jesus said to her, 'Your brother will rise again.' Martha said to him, 'I know that he will rise again in the resurrection on the last day.' Jesus said to her, 'I am the resurrection and the life. Those who believe in me, even though they die, will live, and everyone who lives and believes in me will never die. Do you believe this?' She said to him, 'Yes, Lord, I believe that you are the Messiah, the Son of God, the one coming into the world.'

Following yesterday's discussion with the disciples, Jesus has travelled to the home of Mary and Martha. Lazarus has died and his sisters are deeply distressed. Yet as Jesus sees Martha on the way, she is aware of Jesus' love for her family. At some level she recognises that Jesus is especially close to God. Perhaps if Jesus asks God to raise Lazarus from the dead, God will grant Jesus' request.

Martha misunderstands Jesus' overall purpose: he is the Messiah – God on earth to bring eternal life to all who believe. While Martha has an orthodox belief in the resurrection on the last day, Jesus wants her to know that he is the source of life: more powerful than death itself. Hence anyone who believes in Jesus – who has faith beyond worldly wisdom – will have eternal life: life even following physical death.

Having made this remarkable statement, Jesus asks Martha for a response. Her words are striking. Regardless of limited understanding, Martha's faith has developed from seeing Jesus as close to God to knowing, however tentatively, that Jesus is the promised Messiah. Whether or not she has any idea of the implication of her words, Martha's faith is exemplary.

In the face of the death of a loved one, it is easy to blame God and/or to bargain. Indeed, both are indications of normal grief. Faith in Jesus goes further, seeking to remain with Jesus through death into the future. While grief is the price we pay for love, Jesus, the source of all love, will stay with us as we let go into new life.

'Faith is a footbridge that you don't know will hold you up over the chasm until you're forced to walk out on to it' (Nicholas Wolterstorff).

LAKSHMI JEFFREYS

Preparation

Mary took a pound of costly perfume made of pure nard, anointed Jesus' feet, and wiped them with her hair… But Judas Iscariot… said, 'Why was this perfume not sold for three hundred denarii and the money given to the poor?' (He said this not because he cared about the poor, but because he was a thief; he kept the common purse and used to steal what was put into it.) Jesus said, 'Leave her alone. She bought it so that she might keep it for the day of my burial.'

Tension is increasing as the Pharisees and other leaders seek to arrest and kill Jesus. The astonishment is palpable as discomforted guests at the table with Jesus watch Mary's extravagant and erotic actions. The perfume was worth a year's wages, and no self-respecting woman would dare be seen with her hair down. Such a demonstration of love and humility (washing Jesus' feet) is outrageous.

I wonder if Mary had as little idea of the significance of her actions as Martha in yesterday's reading, when she referred to Jesus as the Messiah. Jesus is in no doubt that Mary is anointing him in preparation for his death, offering selfless love. Judas, on the other hand, sees only wasted money, thereby completely missing who Jesus is.

The focus of world news seems to be economics, and this can blind us to acts of generous love. Within the church we are so often overwhelmed by financial constraints, the requirement to give needing to be balanced against other calls on our limited resources. Mary enacted an intense and beautiful parable which resonates today. A family downsized from a palatial home to a modest semi, giving the proceeds of the sale to needy Christians in other parts of the world. When they were challenged about the seeming unfairness to their children and financial idiocy, they asked the dissenters who was more Christlike in the context of eternity. Seeing and serving Jesus fosters open-handedness and trust in those who are most open to Jesus' love and cynicism in those who are devoted to money.

'Pride in riches… comes not from the Father but from the world. And the world and its desire are passing away, but those who do the will of God live forever' (1 John 2:16–17).

LAKSHMI JEFFREYS

Palm Sunday

The great crowd that had come to the festival heard that Jesus was coming to Jerusalem. So they took branches of palm trees and went out to meet him, shouting, 'Hosanna! Blessed is the one who comes in the name of the Lord – the King of Israel!' Jesus found a young donkey and sat on it; as it is written: 'Do not be afraid, daughter of Zion. Look, your king is coming, sitting on a donkey's colt!'

Following the raising of Lazarus, an increasing number of people follow Jesus. The religious authorities are horrified and seek the death not only of Jesus but also of Lazarus. It is Passover; Jerusalem is heaving with people who are in the city for one of the compulsory visits to the temple. When the pilgrims discover Jesus is on his way into the city, they flock to meet him. Mary expressed exuberant love in private; now the crowd joins in adulation en masse. Martha had acknowledged Jesus was the Messiah, the Son of God; the crowd hails Jesus as the blessed King of Israel, who will free the people of God from their Gentile rulers.

Jesus, again, turns the scene on its head. The king is not mounted on a charger but, as prophesied by Zechariah, sits on a young donkey. 'Hosanna' literally means 'help' or 'save': hence the crowd is calling for help from the one arriving in the name of the Lord, the King of Israel, coming for his people in peace and humility. I wonder how many of those who called out had much idea of what they were saying and doing, the accuracy of their words belying the incomprehension of their minds and hearts.

In our church, as in many, we have Palm Sunday processions, during which we sing seasonal songs and hymns. It is hard not to be swept up in the enthusiasm, even in the village as passers-by gaze in amazement and perhaps embarrassment. We are acknowledging Jesus as king of all, the one who has come to save – not through war but in peace. As I write I think about Christian brothers and sisters across the world, and especially in the Middle East, for whom the cries of 'Hosanna!' have more poignancy.

Lord Jesus, save your people and bring peace.

LAKSHMI JEFFREYS

Betrayal 1

Judas brought a detachment of soldiers together with police from the chief priests and the Pharisees, and they came there with lanterns and torches and weapons. Then Jesus, knowing all that was to happen to him, came forward and asked them, 'For whom are you looking?' They answered, 'Jesus of Nazareth.' Jesus replied, 'I am he.' Judas, who betrayed him, was standing with them. When Jesus said to them, 'I am he', they stepped back and fell to the ground.

Did Judas know what he was doing? Was he merely a pawn in a divine plan? He brought to Jesus a mixture of Gentile soldiers and Jewish leaders, armed with worldly weapons and sources of light. John offers us a glimpse of the world (Jew and Gentile together) who did not believe the Saviour of the world and accept the love and freedom he offered.

Yet Jesus remains supremely in control of the situation. He asks those gathered for whom they are looking, echoing the beginning of John's gospel (see John 1:38). When they answer, 'Jesus of Nazareth', implying some trouble-making rabbi from an insignificant town, Jesus retorts with 'I am he.' 'I am' is the name of the living God: no wonder they step back and fall to the ground. Judas, one who had spent time with Jesus, is standing with them.

Betrayal is always a choice, no matter how limited the options. Judas had spent so much time with Jesus, witnessing miracles ('signs' in John's gospel) but not submitting to Jesus' love. Possibly Jesus did not behave as Judas wanted, leaving the disciple angry and disappointed but unwilling to express this to Jesus. If so, there are many who over the years have felt the same. I think of two women, each of whom has a grandchild with the same life-limiting condition. The women love their grandchildren, but one is increasingly bitter as the youngster fails to live as she thinks a grandchild of hers should. The other woman submits to God's love for her and the child; she is able to express her anger and sadness in prayer, freeing her to love her grandchild without conditions.

If God has angered or disappointed you, tell him – he loves you.

LAKSHMI JEFFREYS

Betrayal 2

Now Simon Peter was standing and warming himself. They asked him, 'You are not also one of his disciples, are you?' He denied it and said, 'I am not.' One of the slaves of the high priest, a relative of the man whose ear Peter had cut off, asked, 'Did I not see you in the garden with him?' Again Peter denied it, and at that moment the cock crowed.

Unlike Judas, Peter shows no signs of being disappointed or angry with Jesus. His denial of Jesus (a form of betrayal) seems to be rooted in fear. Seeking to defend Jesus at his arrest, Peter takes a sword and cuts off the right ear of Malchus, the high priest's slave. Even assuming, as stated in Luke's gospel, that Jesus healed the slave (otherwise Peter would have been arrested there and then), Peter's anxiety in the courtyard is understandable. Yet Peter is not with Jesus, who is being interrogated by the high priest and others. He is terrified of association with Jesus.

The temptation to run away when afraid is immense. Adrenalin is pumping, and the 'flight or fight' response is triggered. Fear is managed with information and reassurance, both of which are available as we stay close to Jesus. Of course, this is counter-intuitive. If Jesus is the cause of the problem, as it seems to Peter, it is madness to be associated with him.

As always, God's ways turn human logic upside down. Jesus has always made it clear that his disciples will face suffering and even death, but that he will be with them by the Holy Spirit. Today across the world individuals and communities are persecuted, sometimes to death, for following Jesus. Faith does not eliminate fear, but remaining with Jesus gives us strength.

There is nothing glamorous about prayer, reading the Bible and giving thanks in all circumstances, alone and with other Christians, but these acts of faithfulness remind believers that the Lord is with them. Next time you are afraid, spend time thanking Jesus for his love for you: your fear will be transformed into praise.

'Perfect love casts out fear' (1 John 4:18). As you pray for Christians persecuted for their faith, ask God to shower them with experiences of his love, despite their circumstances.

LAKSHMI JEFFREYS

Betrayal 3

Pilate… brought Jesus outside and sat on the judge's bench… Now it was the day of Preparation for the Passover; and it was about noon. He said to the Jews, 'Here is your King!' They cried out, 'Away with him! Away with him! Crucify him!' Pilate asked them, 'Shall I crucify your King?' The chief priests answered, 'We have no king but the emperor.' Then he handed him over to them to be crucified.

Many in the crowd had hailed Jesus as the long-awaited king of Israel, sent by God to save God's people. These same individuals now deny they have any king but the emperor and demand of the Roman governor, Pontius Pilate, that Jesus is crucified. Pilate's betrayal of Jesus comes from a combination of fear and unbelief; the crowd's betrayal of Jesus is different. When they thought Jesus was the one they wanted, the crowd adored him. When Jesus demonstrates he will work God's way, not theirs, the crowd reverts to human ideas of power and freedom, choosing the political thug, Barabbas, over the true Saviour. Both the Gentile Pilate and the Jewish crowd choose the wrong king – the earthly, temporary despot – over the creator of the world, bringer of true life.

I am reminded of the prologue at the beginning of John's gospel: 'He was in the world, and the world came into being through him; yet the world did not know him. He came to what was his own, and his own people did not accept him' (1:11–12). The stage is set for God's glory to be revealed in the most horrific and wonderful way.

The 1987 film *The Untouchables* tells the story of how the Chicago gangster Al Capone is brought to justice by federal agent Eliot Ness. During prohibition in America in the 1930s, gangsters run protection rackets, providing the illicit alcohol people want but increasing their power using violence and intimidation. The police, initially seeking to serve the community, are corrupt. The crowd idolise Ness, until he fails to deliver what they want on their terms. Both groups show themselves to be fickle towards the one who can help them.

Be honest: are you part of the crowd?
Has Jesus not lived up to your expectations?

LAKSHMI JEFFREYS

True humility

Jesus knew that his hour had come to depart from this world and go to the Father. Having loved his own who were in the world, he loved them to the end… Jesus, knowing that the Father had given all things into his hands, and that he had come from God and was going to God, got up from the table, took off his outer robe, and tied a towel around himself. Then he poured water into a basin and began to wash the disciples' feet and to wipe them with the towel that was tied around him.

Today is Maundy Thursday. Christian leaders across the world will wash the feet of people in their churches. In England, the monarch (or someone else from the royal household) hands out 'Maundy money' to elderly people, a tradition that dates back to the 17th century. Within my tradition, clergy will renew their ordination vows, with bishops questioned by children. Today, followers of Jesus remember that he came not to be served but to serve. For this reason I unashamedly break from the story of Jesus' death to remember the scene in the upper room.

The symbolism in John's account is profound. Jesus' hour has been mentioned throughout the gospel: it is the time when he is fully revealed as the Saviour of the world, not in glory that humanity would recognise, but on the cross. The watchword of this story is love – Jesus' love for those closest to him before he demonstrates God's love for the whole world. Jesus has nothing to prove. He is fully aware of his purpose and his standing. He has no doubt of his Father's love for him and he knows his ultimate home is in heaven. It is because Jesus knows all of this that he can perform the act of a slave and wash his disciples' feet with profound humility and intimacy.

Jesus is utterly secure in his identity, knowing he is infinitely loved by God. Everything he enacts is performed as loving service, and he wants his followers to do likewise. We can fulfil this call as we receive God's love.

Imagine you are one of the disciples in the upper room.
What is Jesus saying to you as he lovingly washes your feet?

LAKSHMI JEFFREYS

Eternal love

When Jesus saw his mother and the disciple whom he loved standing beside her, he said to his mother, 'Woman, here is your son.' Then he said to the disciple, 'Here is your mother.' And from that hour the disciple took her into his own home. After this, when Jesus knew that all was now finished, he said (in order to fulfil the scripture), 'I am thirsty'... When Jesus had received the wine, he said, 'It is finished.' Then he bowed his head and gave up his spirit.

The theme of love continues. Jesus has been arrested, sentenced to death and subjected to humiliation, and he is now nailed to a cross, dying in agony. Yet as he looks at the disciples gathered at the foot of the cross, he sees two people who have been constant in their love for him. He entrusts his mother to the disciple whom he loved and the disciple to his mother. Thus Jesus forms a new community of believers, built on his love for them.

The greatest act of love is to lay down one's own life for another. In giving up his life for the world, Jesus is showing how much God loves the whole world, revealing God's glory in cosmic terms, focusing on two individuals. Once the community is formed, Jesus' work is done. He announces his thirst, which John writes is 'to fulfil scripture' (though he does not specify which scripture). Then to show that Jesus voluntarily lays down his life and that no one takes it from him, he says, 'It is finished.' He bows his head and gives up his spirit.

Good Friday is often a sombre day. Jesus accomplishes his purpose, giving his life for the world, but there is nothing good about death. God's glory is revealed in sacrificial love, trusting completely in God and thereby able to focus fully on the object of love, the world. Jesus submits to his Father's will, even to death. Surely his loving obedience is the sign of his true kingship, attested to by the sign over his head.

As you think about Jesus' final minutes on the cross, allow God to speak to you of his love and glory. He has called you into a community marked by loving obedience.

'Love so amazing, so divine, demands... my all' (Isaac Watts, 1707).

LAKSHMI JEFFREYS

What next?

Joseph of Arimathea, who was a disciple of Jesus, though a secret one because of his fear of the Jews, asked Pilate to let him take away the body of Jesus... Nicodemus... also came... They took the body of Jesus and wrapped it with the spices in linen cloths, according to the burial custom of the Jews. Now there was a garden in the place where he was crucified, and in the garden there was a new tomb in which no one had ever been laid. And so... they laid Jesus there.

Nicodemus came to Jesus at night (John 3:1–2), fearful of what others would say. Joseph of Arimathea is a secret disciple of Jesus, fearful of the Jews. These two are beginning to recognise who Jesus is and give him a burial appropriate for a king, with spices and a garden tomb. Most striking is that these new disciples of Jesus make themselves known when Jesus has died. What is more, by touching a dead body so close to the sabbath, they make themselves ritually unclean and unable to take part in the feast. They have finally severed links with the religious authorities, who did not acknowledge God's Messiah but instead persecuted him and put him to death. These two men have aligned themselves with Jesus in his death and are about to join the embryonic community of his followers, not knowing what is to come.

We have journeyed with different people who encountered Jesus in the last days of his life. The religious authorities found in Jesus a man who overturned precious ideas and their status. A Samaritan woman, on the other hand, wanted to introduce all the villagers to the one who might be the promised Messiah. Martha, too, spoke about Jesus in these terms, following the death of her brother. Mary was intimate with Jesus, anointing his body for burial, while Jesus was intimate with his disciples, showing them the nature of servant leadership. The crowd, initially looking for a saviour, abandoned Jesus to death when he was not in their image. Judas and Peter betrayed him. Nicodemus, Joseph, Jesus' mother and the beloved disciple formed a community of believers after Jesus' death.

On the eve of Easter Sunday, how do you encounter Jesus?

LAKSHMI JEFFREYS

Easter and beyond in John

 At last the long-anticipated day of resurrection has arrived and the tomb is empty. We may have been getting ready for this day for weeks, but, as George Herbert noted in his poem 'Easter', while we cry, 'Rise heart; thy Lord is risen!', Christ himself was always ahead of us, up by 'break of day' and bringing his 'sweets' along with him.

What 'sweets' would we choose from the giver of life? Perhaps we long to hear him call our name, as he called Mary Magdalene. Or we yearn for reassurance for our fears and doubts like Thomas. Maybe we need to feel the breath of life flowing through us again, revitalising us like the disciples in hiding.

John's gospel introduces the Word made flesh, setting out for us what his earthly life was like and how he changed the lives of others forever. The encounters between Jesus and various characters in John show us what a life of following him might look like, not only then but now in our own time and in our daily lives. Easter is not just a one-day celebration of something that is past, but the yearly acknowledgement that when God raised Jesus from the dead, a new age began, of which we are now a part.

John presents a series of encounters between Jesus and various individuals in his gospel: Andrew, Nicodemus, the man born blind, Lazarus. And this pattern continues after the resurrection. Characters who have become familiar in the body of the gospel story, such as Mary Magdalene, Peter and the beloved disciple, now meet Jesus in his risen body. In these encounters, Jesus always goes beyond their expectations and does something more, and that 'something' still resonates for life in the 21st century. We too are being invited, called to practise the way of self-giving love that sums up Jesus' words and actions in life and death and now in resurrection.

No day can ever be ordinary, because Christ is risen. Learning to trust in the risen Jesus is to know eternal life – life that holds us firm through all our experience, the highs and the lows, and sustains us to our end and beyond.

ELIZABETH HOARE

First Easter

Early on the first day of the week, while it was still dark, Mary Magdalene came to the tomb and saw that the stone had been removed from the tomb. So she ran and went to Simon Peter and the other disciple, the one whom Jesus loved, and said to them, 'They have taken the Lord out of the tomb, and we do not know where they have laid him.'

That first Easter Day did not begin with joy and celebrations. Those came later, but to enter fully into what the first Easter was like, let us imagine the scene described in today's passage.

Mary Magdalene was one of the women who had remained near the cross and watched Jesus die. Now, at the first opportunity the law allowed, she hurried to the tomb to attend to the body, only to find it gone. Her first Easter began with cruel bewilderment added to a grief beyond words. There are echoes of the despair expressed in the Song of Songs: 'I sought him whom my soul loves; I sought him, but found him not' (3:1). Her reaction was to run to the man who had denied Jesus and the mysterious 'disciple whom Jesus loved' to present them with the situation. They were too busy dealing with their own grief and guilt to be able to help, and she was left alone to weep (John 20:11).

Staying with this scene and feeling its impact reminds us that Easter joy is hard-won and goes far beyond the superficial 'happy ending' we rush towards. True Easter joy is something we are invited to discover in the midst of whatever life situation we find ourselves in today. It may be that we have been looking forward to this day and woke up this morning with singing hearts; Easter joy is a crescendo of where we are at this moment. For others it will seem a jarring contradiction to what life feels like, and it will take a determined act of will to celebrate what does not feel to be in harmony with current experience.

God is at work whether or not we can see the evidence at first sight. The realisation that the Lord is risen will come, and its implications will illuminate all of life. Hallelujah!

ELIZABETH HOARE

The dawning of the light

[Mary] turned round and saw Jesus standing there, but she did not know that it was Jesus. Jesus said to her, 'Woman, why are you weeping? For whom are you looking?' Supposing him to be the gardener, she said to him, 'Sir, if you have carried him away, tell me where you have laid him, and I will take him away.' Jesus said to her, 'Mary!' She turned and said to him in Hebrew, 'Rabbouni!'

It is an Easter tradition to reaffirm our baptism vows: 'I turn to Christ.' Twice, in this beautiful scene, Mary turned towards Jesus (vv. 14, 16). As she did so, Jesus was there to greet her and call her by her name, transforming her sorrow into lasting joy.

The artist Rembrandt painted Mary frozen in the moment of her encounter with 'the gardener' and her failure to recognise Jesus. It helps us connect with the slow dawning of the truth in the story. As the dawn broke over Jerusalem, so the gradual dawning of the truth of who was speaking to her hit home. Mary had expected some help finding her beloved Lord's body, but her companions, having failed to locate it, had gone home. She was left alone to grieve his absence and contemplate a future that opened up like an abyss. But Jesus spoke her name, and with that one word, she turned and her life was changed forever. It is one of the most heart-stopping moments in the whole of the New Testament.

John's gospel shows us again and again how the presence of Jesus is transforming. If we let him, he will change us beyond all our expectations in ways that lead to life and true freedom. Like Mary, we hear the Lord calling us by name this side of the resurrection and are invited to walk into a future as people who are recognised, welcomed, cherished and affirmed. Nothing can ever be the same again.

'I have called you by name, you are mine' (Isaiah 43:1). What would it mean in your life this Easter to hear your own name spoken by God and then to reaffirm your baptism vows and turn towards Christ?

ELIZABETH HOARE

Breath of life

Jesus came and stood among them and said, 'Peace be with you.' After he said this, he showed them his hands and his side. Then the disciples rejoiced when they saw the Lord. Jesus said to them again, 'Peace be with you. As the Father has sent me, so I send you.' When he had said this, he breathed on them and said to them, 'Receive the Holy Spirit.'

Peace and purpose, wounds and rejoicing. When we take the risen Jesus seriously and seek to follow him, there are consequences that both comfort and challenge. While we can't share the first disciples' experience of seeing Jesus risen in the flesh knowing he had been sealed up in a tomb three days earlier, we are directly linked to them by the Holy Spirit. For them, fear, then incredulity, turned to joy in a roller coaster of emotions befitting such a cataclysmic series of events. They received his presence in the Holy Spirit to enable them to continue what he had begun. The life that flowed in Jesus' veins is passed on through the life of the Holy Spirit coursing through our being and propelling us out into a world that is crying out for meaning and direction. That same Spirit enables us to live as Easter people just as they did.

Jesus came to them alive, yet bearing the scars of his suffering. The gift of the Spirit was not given without pain, and Easter joy is not guaranteed to be pain-free. We are part of an ongoing story that brings peace and hope to a world full of pain. However small or insignificant our world seems to us, there will be people who need to hear the Easter message, so that they too may be set free from their fears and find hope in their troubles. God the Father sent Jesus, because he loved the world so much, and now Jesus sends his followers in the same way. We can't live up to this in our own strength, but with the Spirit of Jesus himself dwelling in us, we have all the resources we need.

Ask God for what you need to be his presence in your community today.

ELIZABETH HOARE

Doubting faith

Jesus came and stood among them and said, 'Peace be with you.' Then he said to Thomas, 'Put your finger here and see my hands. Reach out your hand and put it in my side. Do not doubt but believe.' Thomas answered him, 'My Lord and my God!' Jesus said to him, 'Have you believed because you have seen me? Blessed are those who have not seen me and yet have come to believe.'

Faith is a gift. So what do we do when it seems that we missed out when it was being distributed? Thomas clearly did not suffer from the FOMO (fear of missing out) that plagues so many today. He had not been present when Jesus first appeared to his disciples huddled together behind locked doors for fear of their lives (20:19–24). As well as not seeing the risen Jesus, Thomas missed out on the gift of the Spirit on that occasion, so he must have felt doubly let down. His defiant response (in 20:25) is just one way human beings try to compensate for feeling inadequate. He had a whole week to nurse his grief and disappointment, a whole week when nothing happened and he could feel vindicated – and then Jesus came again, as he had done before.

This time Jesus paid special attention to the doubting Thomas, and we discover that faith is also a commitment. Picture Thomas' face when Jesus invited him to prod his finger into the recent wounds in his flesh: shame, horror, terror, instantaneous realisation that it really was Jesus and he was alive. Thomas responded in a way that the others present had not, and Jesus then gently draws you and I into the scene, calling us blessed when we believe without having seen the Lord in the flesh.

Most of us struggle to believe at some point, especially when it appears that nothing is happening to confirm the reality of Easter. This encounter shows us that Jesus is still present even when we don't recognise him. It is always his decision to reveal himself when and in whatever way he chooses. It also reminds us that resurrection and cross are inextricably linked.

Meditate today on the way Thomas encountered the risen
yet wounded Christ.

ELIZABETH HOARE

'Come and have breakfast'

When they had gone ashore, they saw a charcoal fire there, with fish on it, and bread. Jesus said to them, 'Bring some of the fish that you have just caught.' So Simon Peter went aboard and hauled the net ashore, full of large fish, a hundred and fifty-three of them; and though there were so many, the net was not torn. Jesus said to them, 'Come and have breakfast.'

Although this is a resurrection scene, it is also so very ordinary. The disciples had returned to their old profession of fishing and the familiar frustration of a night's work with nothing to show for it. Jesus meanwhile got everything necessary for breakfast on the beach apart from the fish. In the verses preceding, John provides so many details to help us picture the scene: Peter putting his clothes back on before leaping into the sea, the distance from the shore and the net groaning yet not torn. Jesus included the disciples in the creation of the scene, urging them to bring some of the fish they had just caught. Then he gave the invitation: 'Come and have breakfast.'

Among the sheer exhilaration of the resurrection and the dramatic appearances of the risen Christ, this one is striking for being low key and almost ordinary. It reminds us that God is in the seeming ordinariness of life as much as, if not more than, the spectacular moments and the ones that fizz. God takes our daily lives and routines and transforms them into signals of grace. They are there to be received, treasured and enlarged in our living every day of our lives.

One of Malcolm Guite's sonnets, 'O Sapientia', ends with an enchanting line asking for an awareness of God's presence in everything. Our world has grown so disenchanted that Easter is now reckoned as a quaint celebration by a minority group of people who still think religion has something to say. No! Easter is God's 'Yes!' to a weary world, where every bush still burns for those with eyes to see.

Our very breath can be to us the presence of the living God,
so ask him for eyes to see and ears to hear that presence
in ordinary ways that throb with life today.

ELIZABETH HOARE

'Do you love me?'

[Jesus] said to him the third time, 'Simon son of John, do you love me?' Peter felt hurt because he said to him the third time, 'Do you love me?' And he said to him, 'Lord, you know everything; you know that I love you.' Jesus said to him, 'Feed my sheep'… After this he said to him, 'Follow me.'

It was only after Easter that Jesus' disciples came to understand what self-giving love really meant. The resurrection illuminated everything else they had experienced of Jesus beforehand. Nevertheless, their recognition that Jesus was alive did not mean that the disciples were suddenly made complete; it would still take a lifetime of following Jesus and practising prayerful reflection. This is a challenge to our instant society. It also challenges our desire for comfort and an easy life, since most of the first disciples, like Simon Peter, had their lives cut short because of their love for Jesus. How did they make that decision day after day to be faithful to their Lord?

Isn't it interesting that Jesus did not ask Simon what his strategic plan was or review his curriculum vitae? He didn't dress him down for his failure to stay with the programme. With Simon Peter, as with every disciple, it is love more than faith, and certainly more than achievement, that Jesus longs to draw forth from us. Simon loved Jesus, and Jesus knew it, but Simon had let him down and denied him. Jesus was giving him the chance to restate his love without the hubris or bravado that had accompanied it before.

Love comes first; then we are invited to follow – whatever that may mean. We do not know where it will lead us, but as the apostle Paul wrote in 1 Corinthians 13, there is no limit to love's faith, hope or endurance, for love never ends.

Like Peter, we are tasked with loving one another so as to be a sign of hope and direction to a lost world. We are not very good at this, as history shows all too clearly, but the desire to fulfil the vision of love is what God is looking for.

Risen Christ, take my feeble love and enable me to play my part in realising your vision of a world renewed.

ELIZABETH HOARE

An ever-deepening experience

Jesus said to him, 'Have you believed because you have seen me? Blessed are those who have not seen and yet have come to believe.' Now Jesus did many other signs in the presence of his disciples, which are not written in this book. But these are written so that you may come to believe that Jesus is the Messiah, the Son of God, and that through believing you may have life in his name.

From first to last, Jesus' life, as portrayed by John, was one of self-giving love. At the end John explains that he has written this way to show what this life meant and how he hopes his readers will respond.

John had spent a lifetime reflecting and interpreting what he had witnessed. This, along with the abiding presence of the risen Jesus, enabled him to gain ever-deeper insights into the meaning of what he wrote. He shared the intimate knowledge of Jesus he had gained, which embraced both memory from the past and ongoing experience in the present. His gospel examines, questions and encounters the nature of the Messiah, and it includes numerous intimate details to flesh out the portrait of someone deeply connected to God and wholly oriented towards others. It is a deeply attractive portrait of what a fully human being looks like.

But clearly there is more. This is the presence we are being invited to get to know and experience for ourselves here and now. John uses words like 'know', 'have' and 'see' to encourage us to experience Jesus in the same way as those who encountered him in his gospel. Our passage talks of having life, and right at the start of the gospel Jesus invites Andrew and his companion to 'come and see' (1:39). When John informs us that he wrote so that we may 'come to believe', he is talking about an ongoing relationship that develops over time and is never completed. To believe is to experience a living, dynamic, growing relationship with Jesus through the Holy Spirit that the Easter God has made possible for us.

Jesus Christ, Son of the living God, deepen my Easter experience
so that my walk with you may ever continue.

ELIZABETH HOARE

Image of the invisible God

When asked 'What does God look like?', children tend to produce something along the lines of an old man with a long beard and a white robe, sitting on a cloud – a slightly more angelic version of Santa Claus. It's interesting to speculate what imagery adults might use, especially if they were unfamiliar with traditional Christian symbolism. The ten commandments included a ban on making images for worship (Exodus 20:4), but most churches are well-endowed with statues, crucifixes, icons or other forms of art, to aid devotion. These figures, depicting Jesus, Mary and assorted saints, offer a variety of ideas about what 'holy people' should look like. Representations of God the Father, however, tend to fall back on the 'old bearded man' theme, while the Holy Spirit rarely appears as anything other than a dove or a flame.

More creative depictions of the members of the Trinity can sometimes be found in story form, offering helpful correctives to all the Victorian blond-haired, blue-eyed stained-glass images of Jesus. One popular example was C.S. Lewis' talking lion Aslan (a Christ figure) in 'The Chronicles of Narnia', who conveyed majesty but also compassion and even playfulness. More recently, William P. Young's *The Shack* surprised many with its bold re-imagining of God the Father as an African-American woman. In this book, Jesus appeared as (less surprisingly) a Middle Eastern carpenter, while the Spirit took the form of an Asian woman.

The gospels record Jesus' statement that 'anyone who has seen me has seen the Father' (John 14:9, NIV), but the Bible includes many more ways of describing God than might emerge from simply reflecting on the person of Jesus of Nazareth. Over the next two weeks, I have selected a variety from across the scriptures, ranging from the impersonal to the highly personal, the consoling to the slightly unsettling. Whatever images of God we prefer, we should remember that God is only ever 'something like' a dove, or a shepherd, or a father. Our God is found in relationship as the Trinity: spoken of as Father, Son and Spirit, yet remaining beyond our understanding. Genesis tells us that we are created 'in the image of God' (1:27). We should resist the temptation to make God in our own image.

NAOMI STARKEY

Shepherd

'This is what the Sovereign Lord says: I myself will search for my sheep and look after them. As a shepherd looks after his scattered flock when he is with them, so will I look after my sheep. I will rescue them from all the places where they were scattered on a day of clouds and darkness. I will bring them out from the nations and gather them from the countries, and I will bring them into their own land... I will tend them in a good pasture, and the mountain heights of Israel will be their grazing land... I myself will tend my sheep and make them lie down.'

We begin with perhaps the most beloved of all pictures, cherished even in contexts far removed from scenes of shepherds walking their flocks through the countryside, trusty dogs at their side. It is the basis of many classic hymns, art and stories, especially for children. I still remember the emotional force of Patricia St John's 1948 book *The Tanglewoods' Secret*, when unhappy runaway Ruth learns of the good shepherd's love and care.

God as shepherd is a picture speaking not only of love and care but guidance and benevolent authority. Psalm 23 (one of the few parts of scripture still widely known beyond the church) describes how the shepherd 'makes' the sheep lie down and 'leads' them to places of refreshment. If they are part of his flock, they are not left to wander aimlessly.

The sheep in our passage from Ezekiel have not simply wandered; they have been scattered by a storm. When bad weather strikes, sheep will huddle wherever they can find shelter, so they may end up stuck on a ledge or (in colder climates) buried in snow. They cannot return to safety on their own but must wait for the shepherd to rescue them. That was the situation for God's people who had been forced into exile – and the wonderful promise is that God the shepherd will find them, bring them home and nurse them back to strength.

'Loving shepherd of Thy sheep, keep Thy lamb, in safety keep;
Nothing can Thy power withstand, none can pluck me from Thy hand'
(Jane Leeson, 1842).

NAOMI STARKEY

Rock

In you, Lord, I have taken refuge; let me never be put to shame; deliver me in your righteousness. Turn your ear to me, come quickly to my rescue; be my rock of refuge, a strong fortress to save me. Since you are my rock and my fortress, for the sake of your name lead and guide me. Keep me free from the trap that is set for me, for you are my refuge. Into your hands I commit my spirit; deliver me, Lord, my faithful God.

Living in Wales, land of both mountains and castles, the combination of 'rock' and 'fortress' in this psalm feels very familiar to me. Even if there's no fortification still standing, names on a map, such as Craig y Ddinas (Fortress Rock), indicate what once stood there. Rocks or mountain tops offer a natural vantage point to keep an eye on what's happening across the surrounding countryside, hence their desirability as castle locations.

Standing on a rock (whether or not in a fortified building), you're less likely to suffer a surprise attack; you're also much safer from natural disasters, such as floods (the image used by Jesus in his parable of the wise and foolish builders, Matthew 7:24–27). The solidity and weightiness of rock and mountains thus make all the more alarming such passages as Psalm 46, which celebrates trust in God 'though the earth give way and the mountains fall into the heart of the sea' (Psalm 46:2).

Throughout the Psalms in particular, we find God referred to as a 'rock' – one who offers strong and sure protection, whether as the foundation for a fortress tower, as a sheltering cleft from the elements or as the solid ground for safe footing when all else is in upheaval. While the idea of God as rock could sound a bit harsh, when life becomes stormy we may find ourselves craving the stability and permanence of rock more than the tranquil comfort of 'green pastures'. And while even the mountains will one day crumble to dust, our God the rock will never fail us.

'Rock of Ages, cleft for me, let me hide myself in Thee'
(Augustus Toplady, 1763).

NAOMI STARKEY

Fire

Now Moses was tending the flock of Jethro his father-in-law, the priest of Midian, and he led the flock to the far side of the wilderness and came to Horeb, the mountain of God. There the angel of the Lord appeared to him in flames of fire from within a bush. Moses saw that though the bush was on fire it did not burn up. So Moses thought, 'I will go over and see this strange sight – why the bush does not burn up.' When the Lord saw that he had gone over to look, God called to him from within the bush, 'Moses! Moses!' And Moses said, 'Here I am.'

The Mount Horeb referred to here may be the same as Sinai, the mountain where Moses mediates the covenant between God and his people. Whatever the exact setting, this fiery meeting takes place in the surrounding wilderness, through which Moses will eventually lead the Israelites in their exodus from Egypt, en route to Canaan.

Fire is one of the basics for human survival, offering warmth, light and a means of cooking food, as well as protection from predators. Used carelessly or maliciously, it can cause terrible destruction, but the fire discovered by Moses is different. Even though it looks like some kind of wildfire, perhaps the result of a lightning strike, miraculously it does not consume the bush as it burns. Maybe this fire is more akin to the blaze of heavenly glory, which scripture describes as associated with God's presence (see Exodus 13, Ezekiel 1 and Matthew 17). As Moses discovers, this burning bush is a place of encounter, not destruction, as the Lord Almighty breaks through into the everyday world of shepherding.

Notice, though, that Moses has to 'go over to look' for encounter to turn into dialogue. His response to the extraordinary spectacle is not fear but curiosity – and his willingness to explore leads to his life-changing commission.

The priest-poet Gerard Manley Hopkins wrote of the world 'charged with the grandeur of God', glory bursting out for those with eyes to see it. How can we be alert to the possibility of such connection?

NAOMI STARKEY

Wind

When the day of Pentecost came, [the disciples] were all together in one place. Suddenly a sound like the blowing of a violent wind came from heaven and filled the whole house where they were sitting. They saw what seemed to be tongues of fire that separated and came to rest on each of them. All of them were filled with the Holy Spirit and began to speak in other tongues as the Spirit enabled them.

Wind and fire: powerful forces of nature which, like so much in the natural world, are capable of harm or healing. Wind can be a cooling breeze or a a vicious hurricane; here the description of a 'violent wind', heralding the coming of the Spirit of God, reminds us that God can be experienced as loving Father but also stern judge. There is fire, too, and then the Spirit fills the believers, literally 'inspiring' them in their utterance to undo the curse of Babel, where humanity was divided by language (Genesis 11:1–9).

The same Hebrew word can mean 'wind', 'breath' or 'spirit', an ambiguity that challenges our tendency to remake God in our own image. On the day of Pentecost, however, God's Spirit comes not in human form – which is possibly what the disciples had been expecting – but signalled by what sounds and looks 'like' wind and flame. In describing the scene, we sense Luke struggling to make sense of spiritual realities beyond comprehension.

The Spirit's coming enables the infant church to begin the task of sharing the good news of salvation with the world, beginning with the pilgrims gathered in Jerusalem for the Pentecost celebrations. Just as wind, rightly harnessed, is a source of renewable energy, so we could describe the Holy Spirit as God endlessly energising us to do God's work, drawing us to share in the ongoing building of the kingdom on earth.

'Jesus said, "Peace be with you! As the Father has sent me,
I am sending you." And with that he breathed on them and said,
"Receive the Holy Spirit"' (John 20:21–22).

NAOMI STARKEY

Light

God is light; in him there is no darkness at all. If we claim to have fellowship with him and yet walk in the darkness, we lie and do not live out the truth. But if we walk in the light, as he is in the light, we have fellowship with one another, and the blood of Jesus, his Son, purifies us from all sin. If we claim to be without sin, we deceive ourselves and the truth is not in us. If we confess our sins, he is faithful and just and will forgive us our sins and purify us from all unrighteousness.

Many of us will know the shock when springtime sun bursts through our windows at a new angle and with a new intensity after the long months of winter shade – and we realise quite how much dust covers the household surfaces! As our passage describes, light lays bare every flaw, every fault, so that speaking of God as 'light' can bring to mind the searching beam of a spotlight as much as a gentle ray of sunshine.

The light that is God exposes us, like the dust from which we were first created, and it would be so much more comfortable to be left discreetly hidden. But God's light shines on us not to sweep us away but to cleanse us and heal us, preparing us to walk in the light with him. Perhaps there are echoes here of Eden (Genesis 3), when God came to walk with the man and the woman, sharing the beauty of the garden, but found them in hiding, ashamed of their disobedience.

Our Bible passage reminds us that we also need the light of God, the light that is God, in our relationships with others. As many a church leader has discovered, some congregations are grimly determined to keep to the shadows, spiritually speaking, clinging on to cobwebby internal politics and power play instead of seeking the richer fellowship that will be theirs if they admit their need of forgiveness and healing – a fellowship in which they will find the very things they seek.

'Light has come into the world, but people loved darkness instead of light because their deeds were evil' (John 3:19).

NAOMI STARKEY

Hiding place

One thing I ask from the Lord, this only do I seek: that I may dwell in the house of the Lord all the days of my life, to gaze on the beauty of the Lord and to seek him in his temple. For in the day of trouble he will keep me safe in his dwelling; he will hide me in the shelter of his sacred tent and set me high upon a rock. Then my head will be exalted above the enemies who surround me; at his sacred tent I will sacrifice with shouts of joy; I will sing and make music to the Lord.

I'd seen 'noddfa', the Welsh word for refuge or safe place, often used as a house name locally, but I hadn't grasped the full force of the word until a church pilgrimage took me into a remote landscape of tiny lanes, scattered farms and small hills. There, on a plateau, we came to a 'noddfa', a standing stone marking the boundary of sanctuary offered by a long-vanished church. According to ancient tradition, anyone managing to reach the 'noddfa' was guaranteed protection.

The sense of hiding place offered in our passage draws on a range of images, including 'rock' as a safe place from which you could check for approaching enemies. We also hear of 'the house of the Lord' and 'his sacred tent', evoking not only the temple in Jerusalem but also the original dwelling place of God with his people: the tabernacle in the wilderness (the same Hebrew word is used for 'tent' and 'tabernacle'). The psalmist's assurance is astonishing: the Lord himself will offer sanctuary in his most holy space. On the 'day of trouble', protection will be freely available to the fugitive: 'shelter first, questions later', we could say.

We see, too, the right response to such welcome. Despite being confident of gaining sanctuary, the psalmist does not take it for granted but overflows with thanksgiving and joy to the one who has saved him. He knows he is safe, but he also knows he is loved.

'The Lord of hosts is with us; the God of Jacob is our refuge'
(Psalm 46:11, NRSV).

NAOMI STARKEY

Bird

At that time Jesus came from Nazareth in Galilee and was baptised by John in the Jordan. Just as Jesus was coming up out of the water, he saw heaven being torn open and the Spirit descending on him like a dove. And a voice came from heaven: 'You are my Son, whom I love; with you I am well pleased.' At once the Spirit sent him out into the wilderness.

The symbolism of different living creatures derives from a variety of cultural memories and assumptions: we speak of a wise owl, man's best friend, the big bad wolf. In many parts of the world, doves are traditionally associated with peace and purity, probably because of their soothing call and white feathers. Maybe that is why the Spirit takes the form of a dove for this post-baptismal moment. Doves (or pigeons) were also acceptable sacrificial gifts according to the Jewish law, being the more affordable option for the poor (such as Mary and Joseph; see Luke 2:24). While we are familiar with the idea of 'lamb of God', we're less likely to think of 'dove of God', yet both creatures served similar purposes in purification rites.

Reading this account of Jesus' baptism, we need to be aware of our own assumptions, because we can overlook the scene's spiritual energy. We can picture something a bit soft-focus – all white wings and gentle light – but being 'descended on' by a bird can be very frightening. We should also note the violence in the description of the heavens being 'torn open'. This is not necessarily a soothing scene; remember that after this, the Spirit who has thus descended sends Jesus out into the wilderness, where he will face physical hardship and temptation.

Something of this slightly alarming energy was captured by the priest-poet R.S. Thomas in his poem 'Raptor', in which God is described as having the characteristics of an owl. This is no wise old bird sitting in a tree but a powerful hunter – and we are in his sights.

'You yourselves have seen… how I carried you on eagles' wings and brought you to myself' (Exodus 19:4).

NAOMI STARKEY

Father

While [the son] was still a long way off, his father saw him and was filled with compassion for him; he ran to his son, threw his arms round him and kissed him. The son said to him, 'Father, I have sinned against heaven and against you. I am no longer worthy to be called your son.' But the father said to his servants, 'Quick! Bring the best robe and put it on him. Put a ring on his finger and sandals on his feet. Bring the fattened calf and kill it. Let's have a feast and celebrate. For this son of mine was dead and is alive again; he was lost and is found.'

Speaking of 'God our Father' is such a familiar part of our worship that we may forget that 'father' is one of many biblical images for God. In recent times, awareness has grown that using the word 'father' can in fact create emotional distance, even fear, in the minds of some, who did not enjoy a positive (or indeed any) relationship with their human fathers.

As with every way of speaking about God, we face the tension of trying to express the inexpressible, but we have in Jesus the one who made explicit the possibility of knowing the Lord God as 'Father': 'No one knows the Son except the Father, and no one knows the Father except the Son and those to whom the Son chooses to reveal him' (Matthew 11:27). In Jesus' revealing of his Father's character, he tells the story of the lost son with its unforgettable climactic scene of the father running to his son, 'while he was still a long way off', to forgive him and bring him home.

Speaking of God as father does not mean he is a remote, chilly figure, making an appearance only to issue rebuke or punishment. It does not mean 'funny old Dad', a benign but largely irrelevant presence at the edge of family life. It means mercy and love; it also means justice and righteousness. Above all, it means one who loves so much, he sent his only Son as Saviour.

'O come to the Father through Jesus the Son' (Fanny Crosby, 1875).

NAOMI STARKEY

Mother

It was I who taught Ephraim to walk, taking them by the arms; but they did not realise it was I who healed them. I led them with cords of human kindness, with ties of love. To them I was like one who lifts a little child to the cheek, and I bent down to feed them… Can a mother forget the baby at her breast and have no compassion on the child she has borne? Though she may forget, I will not forget you!

Conceiving, carrying and giving birth to a child are demanding, life-changing experiences. Raising children to maturity (including the two examples quoted here – teaching them to walk and feeding them as babies) takes much time, patience and energy. The instinctive bond with a birth mother is profound, often retaining significance even when the emotional and hands-on mothering has been done by another since the earliest days.

While the Bible clearly uses maternal imagery for God, calling God 'Mother' has tended to generate unease for some. Calling God 'Father' is not usually equated with saying 'God is male'. Accordingly, the term 'Mother' should not be heard as 'God is female'.

Of course, fathers can be sheltering, nurturing and tender, but scripture also cites such qualities in God using explicitly maternal terms. It is deeply moving to reflect that God's love for us is described as more intense and enduring than a nursing mother's for her baby. In the last 50 or so years, awareness has grown of the need to pay attention to the language we use when talking about God (especially in terms of gender) – and much liturgical creativity has resulted. New prayers, poems and hymns have been composed that draw on the rich biblical store of maternal and feminine imagery for God and have proved transformative for the faith of men and women alike.

'As verily as God is our Father, as verily God is our mother'
(Julian of Norwich, 1342–c. 1416).

NAOMI STARKEY

Gardener

'I am the true vine, and my Father is the gardener. He cuts off every branch in me that bears no fruit, while every branch that does bear fruit he prunes so that it will be even more fruitful. You are already clean because of the word I have spoken to you. Remain in me, as I also remain in you. No branch can bear fruit by itself; it must remain in the vine. Neither can you bear fruit unless you remain in me. I am the vine; you are the branches. If you remain in me and I in you, you will bear much fruit; apart from me you can do nothing.'

Knowing what and when to prune may be a matter of some debate, but confidently wielding the secateurs (or more heavy-duty tools) can transform an unsightly tangle of branches into an attractive corner of the garden. While we may be familiar with the idea of cutting back dead wood, here it's about removing living but less fruitful parts of a plant.

The imagery is rich and complex. The Father is the gardener, working to maximise the vine (Christ's) productivity, which involves shaping us, the branches that should bear fruit (reminding us, perhaps, of the fruit of the Spirit; see Galatians 5:22–23). There's a wonderful interdependency: branches cannot be fruitful without the trunk; a trunk without branches is almost as diminished, although it could grow more branches. Without pruning, growth will be unchecked and eventually strength-sapping: vine and branches need the gardener's care.

The scriptures took shape in a world dominated by subsistence farming, where skilled husbandry meant the difference between thriving and starving. Describing God as a gardener ('smallholder' might be a more accurate term) evokes the image of someone who knows the seasons and soils, who patiently labours in all weathers, whose reward is unlikely to be riches and power but rather food security and a happy family. It evokes humility, commitment, diligence and a thought-provoking contrast to ideas of 'the Lord Almighty'.

'Now the Lord God had planted a garden in the east, in Eden; and there he put the man he had formed' (Genesis 2:8).

NAOMI STARKEY

Bread

Jesus said to them, 'Very truly I tell you, it is not Moses who has given you the bread from heaven, but it is my Father who gives you the true bread from heaven. For the bread of God is the bread that comes down from heaven and gives life to the world.' 'Sir,' they said, 'always give us this bread.' Then Jesus declared, 'I am the bread of life. Whoever comes to me will never go hungry, and whoever believes in me will never be thirsty. But as I told you, you have seen me and still you do not believe.'

Bread is one of the world's staple foods, along with rice and maize, and the sort of bread referred to here was probably what we know as pitta or flat bread. In Jesus' day, it was eaten with every meal and could be used to scoop up other food in the absence of cutlery. With meat a luxury, 'daily bread' (as requested in the Lord's Prayer) meant what you needed to survive. During the Israelites' wilderness wanderings, the Lord provided a miraculous bread substitute, 'manna' (Exodus 16:31), which became a symbol of God's protection and care.

Now Jesus reminds his hearers of that miraculous provision and tells them that in him they will find food to satisfy them forever, heart and soul. This 'food' is still spoken of in terms of the humble loaf, though, rather than the exotic delicacies that would have graced a Roman emperor's table. Jesus comes to meet the needs that we may not even recognise – for forgiveness, healing, transformation – in and through the reality of our daily lives. All we have to do is come as we are and receive with thanksgiving.

The offer is straightforward – too much so for Jesus' hearers, who struggle to believe that the young man standing before them really is God's gift to the world. Even though we know the story of Easter resurrection after the crucifixion, we can still forget to reach out for our risen Saviour's care. Worrying tends to come so much more readily to us than trusting.

'Bread of heaven, feed me till I want no more'
(Williams Pantycelyn, 1717–91).

NAOMI STARKEY

Lamb

Then I saw a Lamb, looking as if it had been slain, standing at the centre of the throne, encircled by the four living creatures and the elders. The Lamb had seven horns and seven eyes, which are the seven spirits of God sent out into all the earth. He went and took the scroll from the right hand of him who sat on the throne. And when he had taken it, the four living creatures and the twenty-four elders fell down before the Lamb. Each one had a harp and they were holding golden bowls full of incense, which are the prayers of God's people.

The final reading in this series, on Saturday, will consider the splendour of heaven's throne room, where the Lord Almighty reigns in majesty, as described in Revelation 4. Today's passage is from the following chapter, where centre stage in that same throne room is an astonishing sight: a lamb 'looking as if it had been slain'. This suggests not the spotless white lamb of so much Christian art but something bloodied, damaged, shocking to behold.

Setting aside the strange apocalyptic language of 'seven horns and seven eyes' (while noting that seven is associated with perfection, perhaps suggesting all-powerful and all-seeing), this is not intended so much as a literal lamb as a drawing together of profound spiritual truths. Here is the Lamb of God, the one who died for the sins of the world and who is now risen to eternal life, present at the centre point of heavenly power and authority. The vulnerable sacrificial victim is heir to the throne of eternal glory, worthy of worship – and worthy to take the scroll from the one seated on that throne, revealing God's purposes for human history.

We are reminded of the Passover, when the blood of lambs was daubed on doorways to protect God's people from the angel of death, as they prepared to escape from Egypt. We are reminded, too, of the last supper, when Jesus took the Passover cup of wine and spoke words of a new covenant, proclaiming a new deliverance, a greater exodus.

'The next day John saw Jesus coming towards him and said, "Look, the Lamb of God, who takes away the sin of the world!"' (John 1:29).

NAOMI STARKEY

Potter

This is the word that came to Jeremiah from the Lord: 'Go down to the potter's house, and there I will give you my message.' So I went down to the potter's house, and I saw him working at the wheel. But the pot he was shaping from the clay was marred in his hands; so the potter formed it into another pot, shaping it as seemed best to him. Then the word of the Lord came to me. He said, 'Can I not do with you, Israel, as this potter does?' declares the Lord.

Watching a skilled potter at work on their wheel, clay taking shape beneath their fingers, is an absorbing experience, as their precision ensures that the jug or bowl or cup grows shapely and strong. Jeremiah the prophet is led to the potter's house and, through what he sees, gains divinely inspired insight into how God is at work in the world.

Even if the clay doesn't mould quite right, the potter is undeterred and simply chooses another shape, making what he can rather than lamenting what he can't do. Thus it is with God: his purposes are unstoppable, although they must still take account of the free will with which God has blessed his creatures. If one way does not work out, another avenue is tried – and it's not a matter of picking a second-rate Plan B because Plan A has failed: God's 'works are perfect, and all his ways are just' (Deuteronomy 32:4). The potter does not give up on the clay; God does not give up on us.

There is a deep security in reflecting how the Lord continues to be at work in and through us. Our heavenly Father is like a patient potter, who works day after day to create beautiful, useful objects from lumps of mud. Like the clay jars and bowls, we are formed by the one who sees us clearly in all our muddiness and knows that we too can be fit for heavenly purpose.

'Yet you, Lord, are our Father. We are the clay, you are the potter; we are all the work of your hand' (Isaiah 64:8).

NAOMI STARKEY

King

There before me was a throne in heaven with someone sitting on it. And the one who sat there had the appearance of jasper and ruby. A rainbow that shone like an emerald encircled the throne. Surrounding the throne were twenty-four other thrones, and seated on them were twenty-four elders. They were dressed in white and had crowns of gold on their heads. From the throne came flashes of lightning, rumblings and peals of thunder. In front of the throne, seven lamps were blazing… Also in front of the throne there was what looked like a sea of glass, clear as crystal.

We come once again to a vision of the throne room of heaven, described by the prophet John. It is a dazzling presentation of kingship beyond any earthly powers and authorities, laden with imagery of precious stones and metals, brilliant light and astonishing purity. This throne room is not the seat of a tyrant, however, because surrounding the seat of power is a rainbow, symbol of God's mercy as promised to Noah, a covenant that 'never again' will floods sweep away all living creatures (Genesis 9:15). Eternal power is tempered with eternal love and forgiveness.

The idea of God's kingship may sit uneasily with us, accustomed as we are to voting for our governments and maintaining the monarchy primarily for ceremonial duties. What we see here, though, must be set alongside all the other images of God on which we have reflected. We worship God Almighty, king of kings, lord of hosts, whom we also experience as tender shepherd, gentle mother, patient potter and the lamb who bears on his risen, glorious body the scars of his cruel death. By that death, we have the right to take our places at the heavenly banquet, sons and daughters of the one seated on the throne.

'God raised us up with Christ and seated us with him in the heavenly realms in Christ Jesus, in order that in the coming ages he might show the incomparable riches of his grace, expressed in his kindness to us in Christ Jesus' (Ephesians 2:6–7).

NAOMI STARKEY

Noah

 The story of Noah runs the risk of being abandoned in the nursery along with beguiling pairs of little wooden animals or pinned forever on the Sunday school board with six-year-olds' rainbow pictures. It is excellent, of course, if Noah can figure early on in our journey of faith, but it is all too easy to overlook the breadth and depth of this bizarre but hugely significant story.

It appears to be an all-or-nothing scenario. When God looks down, he sees nothing but violence, corruption and evil of all kinds – not only in the people's actions but in their very thoughts, the seedbed of their wickedness. He even regrets the day he created them. This is uncomfortable stuff. We prefer to think in shades of grey, that we are all a mix of good and bad – was it really as bad as all that? We can only go by the record of scripture: that the contrast between the depths to which the people had sunk and the heights of the holiness of God meant that judgement was inevitable.

And was the scope of that judgement equally all-embracing? Every living creature? The whole earth? Or just the part of it that was known to the authors at the time? Because it is not possible accurately to date the flood, genealogies often being selective, it's hard to judge the significance of any of the archaeological or geological evidence that has surfaced. Whatever its geographical boundaries, though, this flood was cataclysmic and marked the beginning of a new era in the history of God's plan of redemption.

Redemption, yes: because, as we see at many points throughout scripture, the characteristic way of our gracious God in dealing with evil is both judgement and salvation. This salvation is often of a remnant who have been found faithful and through whom a fresh start is possible, encapsulated in a new form of commitment or covenant between God and his people: 'if you... then I will...' Here, even though he is entrusting responsibility to fallen creatures – Noah is extraordinarily faithful and obedient but not perfect – the new covenant is all from God's side, no conditions imposed. Never again will he visit the earth with wholesale destruction.

SHEILA WALKER

Noah's call

When Lamech had lived for one hundred and eighty-two years, he became the father of a son; he named him Noah, saying, 'Out of the ground that the Lord has cursed this one shall bring us relief from our work and from the toil of our hands.'

The birth of a child cannot but be a hugely significant event, whatever the circumstances: a new, unique life; a new, unique set of possibilities, of doors opening and closing; a destiny as yet known only to God. High-flown words, but perhaps we have glimpsed something of this as we wonder about our new arrivals and how to name them rightly.

A birth in scripture is often the occasion for a prophecy, keeping alive the hope of God's favour and deliverance, which may then be reflected in the name chosen – or given by God – for the child. We see this with Jesus himself, who is so named 'because he will save his people from their sins' (Matthew 1:21; 'Jesus' means 'the Lord saves'). Here the name Noah has the basic meaning of 'rest', but there is a similar verb which has the sense of 'relief' or 'comfort', and his father Lamech picks up on this connection.

How did he know? Was this just a hope for his firstborn or did he have an intuition from God of Noah's future calling? The psalmist reminds us that our days are written in God's book even before we enter this world (Psalm 139:16), and Paul reminds the Turkish Christians that God has prepared beforehand good works for us to undertake (Ephesians 2:10).

Little did Lamech guess, however, the extent of Noah's calling. Where he speaks of 'relief', 'work' and 'toil', God will later speak of 'repentance', 'making' and 'grief': words which echo and strengthen the Hebrew root words of Lamech's prophecy. Noah's call will be much more fundamental and far-reaching than anyone might have imagined. It is all too easy to be satisfied with temporary solutions, papering over cracks, whereas God's purposes involve deep-cleaning, tackling root causes, eliminating the cancer of evil, even when it means death before anything new can emerge.

Gracious God, may I not become too easily satisfied
with less than you intend for me.

SHEILA WALKER

Noah's walk

But Noah found favour in the sight of the Lord. These are the descendants of Noah. Noah was a righteous man, blameless in his generation; Noah walked with God. And Noah had three sons, Shem, Ham and Japheth.

You may know of the experiment in which ten people are asked a yes/no question, the answer to which is obviously 'no'. Nine out of the ten, however, have been primed to say 'yes' and, more often than not, the tenth person, however mystified or reluctant, will agree. It is *so* hard to be the odd one out, to distance yourself from your peers, to challenge the prevailing culture. But Mark Twain once said, 'Whenever you find yourself on the side of the majority, it is time to pause and reflect.'

All credit, then, to Noah. Alone, it seems, in his generation, he is described as righteous, blameless and finding favour with God, a distinction shared by Job and John the Baptist's parents. According to Proverbs, loyalty and faithfulness are the keys to finding favour with God (Proverbs 16:6). It probably didn't make him popular – maybe he was regarded as 'holier than thou', a bit of a goody-goody – but evidently that was a price he was prepared to pay. And what a mercy he did!

'Noah walked with God', as did Enoch; what a great line to have on one's gravestone. The prophet Micah gives us a clue as to what it means to walk with God when he urges Israel to do justice, to love kindness and to walk humbly (Micah 6:8). 'Walking' speaks of our steady progress day by day through life, keeping pace with God, keeping in tune with God. It speaks of the need for consistency, for a sense of direction, for persistence. 'Walking with God' speaks also of companionship, of an intimacy unusual, perhaps, in the Old Testament but recalling the experience of the two disciples on the Emmaus road whose hearts were warmed by the presence of Jesus alongside (Luke 24:32).

Lord, I recognise that being in a minority is rarely comfortable,
but please show me when it may be necessary, and give me grace
to remain faithful in my walk with you.

SHEILA WALKER

Noah's faith

By faith Noah, warned by God about events as yet unseen, respected the warning and built an ark to save his household; by this he condemned the world and became an heir to the righteousness that is in accordance with faith.

'If only…' we might think; if only God would speak to me as clearly as he does so often in the Old Testament. And directly – not always through a prophet, church leader or Christian Book of the Year. Here, just Noah and God: a private conversation.

The fact that God chooses to recognise and confide in Noah sets this story apart from the many Babylonian flood stories with their capricious deities. As when he sends his own Son into the world, God's heart is not to condemn but to save.

Noah must surely have wondered at first if his ears were deceiving him: miles from the sea, not a cloud in the sky, and he was to build an enormous boat. Even if he was aware of the precarious state of the nation, and the likelihood therefore of God's judgement in some way, this must have seemed an extraordinary commission. Maybe it is the amount of detail that convinces him he is indeed hearing aright and enables him to respond with the faith that expresses itself in obedience.

Obedience – because faith is more than simply the belief that amounts to a set of ideas with which we can agree. Only when that belief results in action – and often action which would have been unthinkable without trusting in the leading and enabling of God – can it be counted as the faith which amounts to righteousness in the sight of God. And this is the faith which speaks to others: they are usually less interested in our ideas, more in the way we live our lives. How far do our lives attract or repel others? Noah's actions could not help but provoke a response, whether of ridicule or amazement; either way, the people's lack of connection with God is shown up, hence condemned.

How far are we willing to 'stand out' as Christians?
What might be the temptations? The risks? The benefits?

SHEILA WALKER

Noah's ark

'Make yourself an ark of cypress wood; make rooms in the ark, and cover it inside and out with pitch. This is how you are to make it: the length of the ark three hundred cubits, its width fifty cubits, and its height thirty cubits.'

It seems that the Almighty errs on the side of utilitarian rather than luxurious when it comes to waterborne transport (Jonah might agree). Spacious, yes: considerably longer than a football pitch, this ark, and only eight people on board. But then there is a veritable menagerie to crowd the decks with noise, smells, droppings and every kind of challenge to whatever farming skills Noah and his family may have had.

A similar Egyptian root word for 'ark' has the meaning 'coffin'. There is a sense in which Noah's family, entombed in the ark for over a year, will then be saved through the flood waters, finding new life through this 'death': an image which Peter, in his first letter, will apply to the waters of baptism (1 Peter 3:20–21). It is interesting, too, that the word for 'pitch' is the same as that for 'atonement': the root meaning being 'to cover'. Just as the ark is covered, sealed with pitch, and the family 'sealed in' by God, so our new life is enabled and protected by the atoning sacrifice of Jesus.

'How much longer, Lord?' Imagine Noah looking out each morning, only to be faced with 40 days of rain, 150 of rising water and many months more before the water subsides. Even then, he doesn't rush things, desperate though they must have been by then to set foot on terra firma; no, he waits for the dove to bring an olive leaf. What patience, what trust in the wisdom and timing of God!

'How much longer, Lord?' The question re-echoes today in so many places, with so many people suffering from floods or drought, violence or homelessness and dozens of species of plants and animals becoming extinct every day, largely due to irresponsible human activity. 'How much longer, Lord?' Their 'ark' – their provision, protection, salvation – takes a somewhat different form today, mediated through all kinds of relief organisations.

Lord, help me to play my part in caring for your creation, through my lifestyle choices and through giving, lobbying and prayer.

SHEILA WALKER

Noah's fall

Noah, a man of the soil, was the first to plant a vineyard. He drank some of the wine and became drunk, and he lay uncovered in his tent. And Ham, the father of Canaan, saw the nakedness of his father, and told his two brothers outside. Then Shem and Japheth took a garment, laid it on both their shoulders, and walked backwards and covered the nakedness of their father; their faces were turned away, and they did not see their father's nakedness. When Noah awoke from his wine and knew what his youngest son had done to him, he said, 'Cursed be Canaan.'

It's always a relief to know that even the great heroes of the Bible were not perfect: Noah, David, Solomon. If indeed Paul is right that all have sinned and fall short of the glory of God (Romans 3:23), we must assume that even the likes of Enoch and Daniel must have had their occasional glitch. It is possible, if Noah was indeed the first to embark on viniculture, that he was unfamiliar with the dangers of excess – though, unlike many of us, he seems to have made no excuses for himself. Ignorance, in any case, then as now, does not generally constitute a defence in law.

Noah's 'fall' and subsequent need for covering echoes that original fall in Genesis 3, when nakedness becomes a cause of shame and God provides covering for Adam and Eve. From now on, every new beginning will yet carry the seeds of failure, as Noah and Ham carry the sin of the antediluvian world into the new one. Despite Noah's building of an altar and enjoying the blessing of God, human nature is now inherently flawed; all are now 'east of Eden' and nothing short of total death will suffice to change things.

Though there is no moral comment on Noah's drunkenness, inevitably there are implications. His sons' response is mixed, and Ham's lack of respect has consequences: Canaan is cursed and will become an ongoing source of temptation to Israel to abandon God – their Father and their father's God – in favour of idols.

---

*How often do we need reminding that we are called not to judge,
but to cover one another's weaknesses, mindful of our own?*

SHEILA WALKER

Noah's arc

'I have set my bow in the clouds, and it shall be a sign of the covenant between me and the earth. When I bring clouds over the earth and the bow is seen in the clouds, I will remember my covenant that is between me and you and every living creature of all flesh; and the waters shall never again become a flood to destroy all flesh.'

The rainbow is used by many charities and organisations as their symbol, including gay pride, a bus company, a trust for children with life-threatening illnesses and many more, always with the aim of capturing a sense of celebration, joy and hope. As usual, God was there first, greeting his newly washed world with a burst of colour and a covenant promise.

And what a promise! It is made to every living creature, unconditionally and for all time; God lays aside his battle bow and replaces it with a sign that, behind and beyond every dark rain cloud, his sun continues to shine and will break through.

Again we see that God's judgements are tempered with mercy: while he does not always dispel the dark clouds – indeed, he may send them – disaster will never again be all-encompassing. Suffering will continue to be part of the lot of all creation, as will both sun and storm, but localised. This is the first of the four great Old Testament covenants – with Noah, Abraham, the Israelites and King David – all of which seek to establish a relationship of commitment between God and his chosen people, a relationship into which he can eventually invite everyone, by way of the cross of Christ.

We are reminded again that we are one with the whole of creation, interdependent and co-recipients of God's promises. It may seem strange that God should need something to jog his memory in times of judgement; maybe it is we who should take the sign of the rainbow as a reminder of the seriousness of ignoring his commands, abusing his world and taking for granted his grace.

Lord, help us, as Christians, to remember, to recapture and to share the full significance of the rainbow as a symbol of our faith in God's covenant.

SHEILA WALKER

Reading *New Daylight* in a group

SALLY WELCH

I am aware that although some of you cherish the moments of quiet during the day which enable you to read and reflect on the passages we offer you in *New Daylight*, other readers prefer to study in small groups, to enable conversation and discussion and the sharing of insights. With this in mind, here are some ideas for discussion starters within a study group. Some of the questions are generic and can be applied to any set of contributions within this issue; others are specific to certain sets of readings. I hope they generate some interesting reflections and conversations!

General discussion starters

These can be used for any study series within this issue. Remember there are no right or wrong answers – these questions are simply to enable a group to engage in conversation.

- What do you think is the main idea or theme of the author in this series? Do you think they succeeded in communicating this to you, or were you more interested in the side issues?

- Have you had any experience of the issues that are raised in the study? How have they affected your life?

- What evidence does the author use to support their ideas? Do they use personal observations and experience, facts, quotations from other authorities? Which appeals to you most?

- Does the author make a 'call to action'? Is that call realistic and achievable? Do you think their ideas will work in the secular world?

- Can you identify specific passages that struck you personally – as interesting, profound, difficult to understand or illuminating?

- Did you learn something new reading this series? Will you think differently about some things, and if so, what are they?

Questions for specific series

Psalms 29—42 – Ross Moughtin

Ross claims that 'we've been made with a facility to share our lives with God'. How does that facility manifest itself for you? Do you find it easy to share your life with God? In what ways do you do so? Are there parts of your life that you do not share with God, or that you would prefer God had no part in? Does this arise from our complacency or our fear?

Dear divided church: 1 Corinthians – Terry Hinks

'The Spirit that searches the very depths of God is also the Spirit that searches our depths, showing us who we really are and who we might become, by the grace of God.' How would you define the Holy Spirit? How might it reveal who you are – and who you might become?

Esther – Sally Welch

Which of these reflections have you found most challenging and why? Are there lessons for us in the way Esther behaves, or is the story too tied up with its time and customs?

The book of Esther never mentions God – is it possible to be a Christian and never talk about Christ?

In her reflections, Naomi Starkey looks at the different images of God we are given in the Bible. They range from gardener and shepherd to fire and lamb, with the final image that of a being with 'the appearance of jasper and ruby', surrounded by a rainbow (Revelation 4:3, NIV).

Which image of God most appeals to you? Which do you find least sympathetic? How do the different images presented by Naomi affect your understanding of God?

Meet the author: Terry Hinks

Terry, you studied theology at Oxford. What was that experience like for you?

Three years at Mansfield College, Oxford, was a stimulating and stretching experience, with the Bible coming alive in new ways. Alongside the academic approach were some fascinating placements; the year with a Reading church kept me grounded. And best of all, I met my wife, Elizabeth, at the college.

You have ministered in both rural and urban contexts – do you see many differences?

Communities and church cultures vary greatly, each with their strengths and weaknesses. My longest ministry was in Romsey – a market town with a great community spirit – alongside a small village church full of characters. My present churches in High Wycombe and Bourne End bring new opportunities and challenges, especially in the area of service to the most vulnerable and deprived and in relationship to other faith traditions. A constant in all my ministries has been the value of working with Christians of many different backgrounds and perspectives.

How did you begin as a writer? How do you get your inspiration?

A workshop led by Kate Compston (a URC minister and writer) in Windermere 30 years ago set me going. Kate helped a group of us reflect deeply on a Bible text, gather diverse thoughts and reactions and then write a prayer arising from this. Through a sabbatical in 2007 I began to write on praying with the gospels, resulting in a number of publications, the most recent being *Praying the Way: With Matthew, Mark, Luke and John* (BRF, 2018).

Who has inspired you in your life?

Nowadays my two children (grown-up and married) regularly inspire me with their enthusiastic and determined approach to life. In terms of the Christian way, the late Michael Mayne has been a great inspirer. Our paths crossed on several occasions in my life and ministry, and his writing has been a source of huge encouragement and enjoyment, especially *This Sunrise of Wonder* (Fount, 1995). Artists such as Stanley Spencer (1891–1959) have also enriched my view of life and faith. Stanley lived and worked in Cookham, just a few miles from where I live now.

Recommended reading

Lent is not about giving up or taking up, but a radical opening up: the opening up of our lives to God's transformative kingdom. That is the challenge Trystan Owain Hughes sets in *Opening Our Lives*, BRF's Lent book for 2021. Through practical daily devotions he calls on us to open our eyes to God's presence, our ears to his call, our hearts to his love, our ways to his will, our actions to his compassion and our pain to his peace.

TRYSTAN OWAIN HUGHES

OPENING OUR LIVES

Devotional readings for Lent

BRF LENT BOOK

The following is an edited extract from a reading entitled 'Our call to recognise Jesus in ourselves', reflecting on Galatians 3:23–29.

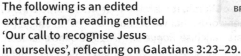

Recently, I officiated at the funeral of a congregation member. Derek was such a lovely man. He was a quiet and modest character. I thought I knew him well, but it was only when I visited him at home a few months before his passing that I heard more about his life. It was then I realised the quiet, and quite beautiful, impact that Derek's faith had on him and subsequently on the world around him. He was working in sales in the Welsh steel industry when he won a scholarship with his company to undertake community work in Austria to build houses for refugees. He then returned to the UK to supervise the refurbishment of a school building for refugee children. After that, he felt he had a calling to work in the social work field, so he joined the Probation Service and remained there for the rest of his working life. Derek's impact on the young people on probation he helped went far beyond his own experience. In fact, I spoke to a number of people attending his funeral who, unbeknown to Derek himself, had completely turned their lives around due to his kind and caring influence.

Not all of us can leave such an evident impact on the lives of those around us. However, our faith should still be having a positive and loving effect on everyday situations, on the world around us and on the people with whom we come into contact. In our passage today, Paul reminds us of our radical call to live lives that reflect the life of Jesus. The uniqueness of first-century Christian baptism was that, as our passage states, converts were baptised 'into Christ'. The Jewish conversion ritual had no equivalent language. Paul is clear that, in baptism, we not only become one with each other, but also with Jesus.

A few years back, I attended a service in Llandaff Cathedral in Cardiff to celebrate 20 years of women priests in Wales. The preacher asked us to turn to the person next to us and trace the shape of the cross on their forehead. It was hugely moving, as it reminded us of our baptism and our calling to live as Christ did – bringing hope to our communities, peace to people's hearts and compassion to those who are suffering. We are, in baptism, marked with a cross, and, while people can't see the actual cross that was left on our foreheads with oil and water in our baptism, they should see that cross reflected in our daily lives.

In the Eastern Orthodox Church, it is stated that we become *christoi* through baptism – in other words, that we become 'Christs'. In one of the recent films in the Star Wars franchise, *Rogue One* (2016), a blind character, Chirrut Îmwe, relies on the Force to know when to shoot or to avoid bullets. He repeats a phrase continually: 'The Force is in me; I am in the Force.' As I sat and watched the film in the cinema, I was amazed to hear that phrase, because it is reminiscent of a meditation I have used for many years to remind me of my call to live out Jesus in my everyday actions – 'Christ is in me; I am in Christ.' That is, in a nutshell, what being called by Jesus is all about.

Yesterday we considered the challenge to see Jesus in other people. Today, though, we are reminded that, by how we act and by what we do, people will see Jesus in us. We will be, as today's passage puts it, 'clothed' with Christ. As such, while there is certainly a place for talking about faith and discussing doctrine, in reality we connect with people in a far more profound way by reflecting Jesus in our acts of compassion and our seemingly inconsequential words and deeds of kindness.

When I left my childhood home to go to university to study theology, my dad gave me his Bible – it was the Bible that had been given to him by his own father when he had left for theological college. Inside the Bible were scribbled these words: 'Don't become of so much heavenly value that you are of no earthly use.' Our call to live out the gospel each day is at the very heart of our faith. As Albert Schweitzer put it, on reflecting on his Christian ministry as a medic:

> I wanted to be a doctor that I might be able to work without having to talk. For years I have been giving myself out in words… This new form of activity I could not represent to myself as being talking about the religion of love, but only as an actual putting it into practice.

A prayer to be prayed slowly and mindfully – allow each word and phrase to inspire your walk with God:

Lord Jesus,
You call us to become more like you,
Transform us into your likeness by helping us to recognise ways we can reflect your love,
While not all of us can do great things, in you all of us can do things with great love,
In your name,
Amen

To order a copy of this book, please use the order form on page 149 or visit **brfonline.org.uk**.

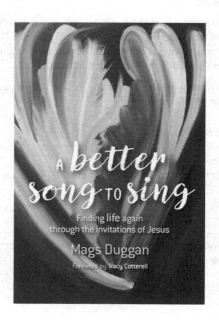

Many followers of Jesus are quietly desperate for more than they are currently experiencing. That more is found as we respond to the invitations of Jesus, which hold out to us the hope of a truly vibrant, transformed life – a better song to sing. Each chapter of this book explores one invitation, drawing out its possible implications for our lives and suggesting a spiritual practice or reflection to help us ground that invitation in our present-day reality.

A Better Song to Sing
Finding life again through the invitations of Jesus
Mags Duggan
978 0 085746 005 8 £8.99
brfonline.org.uk

Develop a pattern of Bible reading, reflection & prayer

Come & See

Learning from the life of Peter

Stephen Cottrell

When we look at the life of Peter – fisherman, disciple, leader of the church – we find somebody who responded wholeheartedly to the call to 'come and see'. Come and meet Jesus, come and follow him, come and find your life being transformed. *Come and See* provides a pattern of Bible reading, reflection and prayer based on the story of Peter, plus comment and questions for personal response or group discussion.

Come and See
Learning from the life of Peter
Stephen Cottrell
978 1 80039 019 5 £8.99
brfonline.org.uk

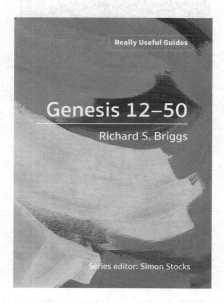

Really Useful Guides

Genesis 12–50

Richard S. Briggs

Series editor: Simon Stocks

Each Really Useful Guide focuses on a specific biblical book, making it come to life for the reader, enabling them to understand the message and to apply its truth to today's circumstances. Though not a commentary, it gives valuable insight into the book's message. Though not an introduction, it summarises the important aspects of the book to aid reading and application.

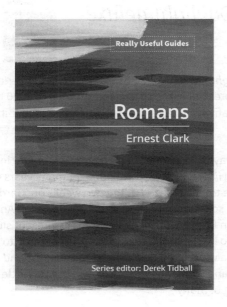

Enjoy a little luxury: upgrade to *New Daylight deluxe*

New Daylight has long been BRF's most popular series of Bible reading notes but in the spring and summer of 2020 the number of appreciative messages leapt. This, from a reader in Zurich, is typical:

> 'We always find inspiration and encouragement in reading *New Daylight* which we have done for many years now. However we were totally amazed at the two weeks on 'Gardens in the Bible'... so relevant to the present – wonderful! And now the series on Ezekiel. Again spoken into the present situation. How timely to be reminded that we should continue to live our lives in such a way as will be a witness to those around us. With many thanks and with prayer that God will use this little booklet to the blessing of many.'

Many readers enjoy the compact format of the regular *New Daylight* but more and more people are discovering the advantages of the larger format, premium edition, *New Daylight deluxe*. The pocket-sized version is perfect if you're reading on the move but the larger print, white paper and extra space to write your own notes and comments all make the deluxe edition an attractive alternative and significant upgrade.

Why not try it to see if you like it? You can order single copies at brfonline.org.uk/newdaylightdeluxe

To order

Online: **brfonline.org.uk**
Telephone: +44 (0)1865 319700
Mon–Fri 9.15–17.30

Delivery times within the UK are
normally 15 working days. Prices are
correct at the time of going to press
but may change without prior notice.

Title	Price	Qty	Total
Seven Sacred Spaces	£10.99		
The Bible Doesn't Tell Me So	£8.99		
Opening Our Lives (BRF Lent book)	£8.99		
A Better Song to Sing	£8.99		
Come and See	£8.99		
Really Useful Guides: Genesis 12—50; Romans – available on Kindle only at amazon.co.uk			

POSTAGE AND PACKING CHARGES			
Order value	UK	Europe	Rest of world
Under £7.00	£2.00		
£7.00–£29.99	£3.00	Available on request	Available on request
£30.00 and over	FREE		

Total value of books	
Postage and packing	
Total for this order	

Please complete in BLOCK CAPITALS

Title _____ First name/initials _____ Surname _____

Address _____

_____ Postcode _____

Acc. No. _____ Telephone _____

Email _____

Method of payment

☐ Cheque (made payable to BRF) ☐ MasterCard / Visa

Card no. ☐☐☐☐ ☐☐☐☐ ☐☐☐☐ ☐☐☐☐

Expires end ☐☐ M M ☐☐ Y Y   Security code* ☐☐☐   Last 3 digits on the reverse of the card

Signature* _____ Date _____ /_____ /_____
*ESSENTIAL IN ORDER TO PROCESS YOUR ORDER

Please return this form to:

BRF, 15 The Chambers, Vineyard, Abingdon OX14 3FE | enquiries@brf.org.uk
To read our terms and find out about cancelling your order, please visit **brfonline.org.uk/terms**.

The Bible Reading Fellowship (BRF) is a Registered Charity (233280)

ND0121

BRF needs you!

If you're one of our many thousands of regular *New Daylight* readers, you will know all about the impact that regular Bible reading has your faith and the value of daily notes to guide, inform and inspire you.

Here are some recent comments from *New Daylight* readers:

> 'Thank you for all the many inspiring writings that help so much when things are tough.'

> 'Just right for me – I learned a lot!'

> 'We looked forward to each day's message as we pondered each passage and comment.'

If you have similarly positive things to say about *New Daylight*, would you be willing to share your experience with others? Perhaps you could give a short talk or write a brief article about why you find *New Daylight* so helpful. You could form a *New Daylight* reading group, perhaps supplying members with their first copy of the notes. Or you could pass on your back copies or give someone a gift subscription. However you do it, the important thing is to find creative ways to put a copy of *New Daylight* into someone else's hands.

It doesn't need to be complicated and we can help with group and bulk buy discounts.

We can supply further information if you need it and would love to hear about it if you do find ways to get *New Daylight* into new readers' hands.

For more information:

- Email **enquiries@brf.org.uk**
- Telephone BRF on +44 (0)1865 319700 Mon–Fri 9.15–17.30
- Write to us at BRF, 15 The Chambers, Vineyard, Abingdon OX14 3FE

Enabling all ages to grow in faith

At BRF, we long for people of all ages to grow in faith and understanding of the Bible. That's what all our work as a charity is about.

- Our **Living Faith** ministry offers resources helps Christians go deeper in their understanding of scripture, in prayer and in their walk with God. Our conferences and events bring people together to share this journey, while our Holy Habits resources help whole congregations grow together as disciples of Jesus, living out and sharing their faith.

- We also want to make it easier for local churches to engage effectively in ministry and mission – by helping them bring new families into a growing relationship with God through **Messy Church** or by supporting churches as they nurture the spiritual life of older people through **Anna Chaplaincy**.

- Our **Parenting for Faith** team coaches parents and others to raise God-connected children and teens, and enables churches to fully support them.

Do you share our vision?

Though a significant proportion of BRF's funding is generated through our charitable activities, we are dependent on the generous support of individuals, churches and charitable trusts.

If you share our vision, would you help us to enable even more people of all ages to grow in faith? Your prayers and financial support are vital for the work that we do. You could:

- Support BRF's ministry with a regular donation;
- Support us with a one-off gift;
- Consider leaving a gift to BRF in your will (see page 152);
- Encourage your church to support BRF as part of your church's giving to home mission – perhaps focusing on a specific ministry or programme;
- Most important of all, support BRF with your prayers.

Donate at **brf.org.uk/donate** or use the form on pages 153–54.

There is a time for everything...

There is a time for everything, and a season for every activity under the heavens: a time to be born and a time to die... a time to kill and a time to heal, a time to tear down and a time to build, a time to weep and a time to laugh...
ECCLESIASTES 3:1–4 (NIV, abridged)

I feel intimidated by the task before me: writing something now, in mid-June, that will still be of substance when you read it early next year. Yet, I have good cause for confidence.

While coronavirus has affected us all, some in ways that will never be forgotten, there is comfort to be found in the words of scripture. Ecclesiastes tells us that there is a time for everything – a season comes, and a season goes. Jesus warns us not to store up treasures for ourselves on earth, but rather to place our hope fully in the heavenly kingdom, where good things do not end and where every tear is wiped away.

These truths do not remove the pain we feel now. They do give hope beyond it.

Our work as a charity is to share timeless truths and an unswerving hope with a constantly changing world – work that requires we adapt to make a difference in every generation.

Much of what we do today – and God willing into the future – is funded by donations and gifts in wills.

I'd like to invite you to prayerfully consider whether you could support this work through a gift in your will. If you would like further information about leaving a gift in your will to BRF, please get in touch with us on **+44 (0)1235 462305**, via **giving@brf.org.uk** or visit **brf.org.uk/lastingdifference**.

Martin Gee
Fundraising manager

PS: Please be assured that whatever decision you reach about your will, you don't need to tell us and we won't ask. May God grant you wisdom as you reflect on these things.

> Pray. Give. Get involved.
> **brf.org.uk**

SHARING OUR VISION – MAKING A GIFT

I would like to make a gift to support BRF. Please use my gift for:

☐ Where it is most needed ☐ Anna Chaplaincy ☐ Living Faith
☐ Messy Church ☐ Parenting for Faith

Title	First name/initials	Surname

Address

	Postcode

Email

Telephone

Signature	Date

giftaid it You can add an extra 25p to every £1 you give.

Please treat as Gift Aid donations all qualifying gifts of money made

☐ today, ☐ in the past four years, ☐ and in the future.

I am a UK taxpayer and understand that if I pay less Income Tax and/or Capital Gains Tax in the current tax year than the amount of Gift Aid claimed on all my donations, it is my responsibility to pay any difference.

☐ My donation does not qualify for Gift Aid.

Please notify BRF if you want to cancel this Gift Aid declaration, change your name or home address, or no longer pay sufficient tax on your income and/or capital gains.

We will use your personal data to process this transaction. From time to time we may send information about the work of BRF that we think may be of interest to you. Our privacy policy is at **brf.org.uk/privacy**. Please contact us if you wish to discuss your mailing preferences.

Please complete other side of form ➲

SHARING OUR VISION – MAKING A GIFT

Regular giving

By Direct Debit: You can set up a Direct Debit quickly and easily at **brf.org.uk/donate**

By Standing Order: Please contact our Fundraising Administrator +44 (0)1865 319700 | **giving@brf.org.uk**

One-off donation

Please accept my gift of:

☐ £10 ☐ £50 ☐ £100 Other £ ☐

by (*delete as appropriate*):

☐ Cheque/Charity Voucher payable to 'BRF'

☐ MasterCard/Visa/Debit card/Charity card

Name on card

Card no. ☐☐☐☐ ☐☐☐☐ ☐☐☐☐ ☐☐☐☐ ☐☐☐☐

Expires end [M][M] [Y][Y] Security code* ☐☐☐

*Last 3 digits on the reverse of the card
ESSENTIAL IN ORDER TO PROCESS YOUR PAYMENT

Signature   Date

☐ I would like to leave a gift to BRF in my will. Please send me further information.

For help or advice regarding making a gift, please contact our Fundraising Administrator +44 (0)1865 319700

↻ Please complete other side of form

Registered with

FR
FUNDRAISING
REGULATOR

Please return this form to:
BRF, 15 The Chambers, Vineyard, Abingdon OX14 3FE

The Bible Reading Fellowship is a Registered Charity (233280)

BRF

NEW DAYLIGHT SUBSCRIPTION RATES

Please note our new subscription rates, current until 30 April 2022:

Individual subscriptions
covering 3 issues for under 5 copies, payable in advance
(including postage & packing):

	UK	Europe	Rest of world
New Daylight	£18.00	£25.95	£29.85
New Daylight 3-year subscription (9 issues) (not available for Deluxe)	£52.65	N/A	N/A
New Daylight Deluxe per set of 3 issues p.a.	£22.35	£32.55	£38.55

Group subscriptions
covering 3 issues for 5 copies or more, sent to one UK address (post free):

New Daylight	£14.25 per set of 3 issues p.a.
New Daylight Deluxe	£17.85 per set of 3 issues p.a.

Please note that the annual billing period for group subscriptions runs from 1 May to 30 April.

Overseas group subscription rates
Available on request. Please email **enquiries@brf.org.uk**.

Copies may also be obtained from Christian bookshops:

New Daylight	£4.75 per copy
New Daylight Deluxe	£5.95 per copy

> All our Bible reading notes can be ordered online by visiting
> **brfonline.org.uk/collections/subscriptions**
>
> *New Daylight* is also available as an app for
> Android, iPhone and iPad
> **brfonline.org.uk/collections/apps**

NEW DAYLIGHT INDIVIDUAL SUBSCRIPTION FORM

All our Bible reading notes can be ordered online by visiting
brfonline.org.uk/collections/subscriptions

☐ I would like to take out a subscription:

Title _____ First name/initials _____ Surname _____

Address _____

_____ Postcode _____

Telephone _____ Email _____

Please send *New Daylight* beginning with the May 2021 / September 2021 /
January 2022 issue (*delete as appropriate*):

(please tick box)	UK	Europe	Rest of world
New Daylight 1-year subscription	☐ £18.00	☐ £25.95	☐ £29.85
New Daylight 3-year subscription	☐ £52.65	N/A	N/A
New Daylight Deluxe	☐ £22.35	☐ £32.55	☐ £38.55

Total enclosed £ _____ (cheques should be made payable to 'BRF')

Please charge my MasterCard / Visa ☐ Debit card ☐ with £ _____

Card no. ☐☐☐☐ ☐☐☐☐ ☐☐☐☐ ☐☐☐☐

Expires end ☐☐ ☐☐ Security code* ☐☐☐ Last 3 digits on the reverse of the card

Signature* _____ Date _____/_____/_____

*ESSENTIAL IN ORDER TO PROCESS YOUR PAYMENT

To set up a Direct Debit, please also complete the Direct Debit instruction on page 159
and return it to BRF with this form.

Please return this form with the appropriate payment to:
BRF, 15 The Chambers, Vineyard, Abingdon OX14 3FE

To read our terms and find out about cancelling your order,
please visit **brfonline.org.uk/terms**.

ND0121

NEW DAYLIGHT GIFT SUBSCRIPTION FORM

☐ I would like to give a gift subscription (please provide both names and addresses):

Title .... First name/initials .... Surname ....

Address ....

.... Postcode ....

Telephone .... Email ....

Gift subscription name ....

Gift subscription address ....

.... Postcode ....

Gift message (20 words max. or include your own gift card):

....

....

Please send *New Daylight* beginning with the May 2021 / September 2021 / January 2022 issue (*delete as appropriate*):

(*please tick box*)	UK	Europe	Rest of world
New Daylight 1-year subscription	☐ £18.00	☐ £25.95	☐ £29.85
New Daylight 3-year subscription	☐ £52.65	N/A	N/A
New Daylight Deluxe	☐ £22.35	☐ £32.55	☐ £38.55

Total enclosed £ .... (cheques should be made payable to 'BRF')

Please charge my MasterCard / Visa ☐ Debit card ☐ with £ ....

Card no. ☐☐☐☐ ☐☐☐☐ ☐☐☐☐ ☐☐☐☐

Expires end ☐☐ ☐☐ Security code* ☐☐☐ Last 3 digits on the reverse of the card

Signature* .... Date ...... /...... /......

*ESSENTIAL IN ORDER TO PROCESS YOUR PAYMENT

To set up a Direct Debit, please also complete the Direct Debit instruction on page 159 and return it to BRF with this form.

Please return this form with the appropriate payment to:
BRF, 15 The Chambers, Vineyard, Abingdon OX14 3FE

To read our terms and find out about cancelling your order, please visit **brfonline.org.uk/terms**.

The Bible Reading Fellowship is a Registered Charity (233280)

DIRECT DEBIT PAYMENT

You can pay for your annual subscription to our Bible reading notes using Direct Debit. You need only give your bank details once, and the payment is made automatically every year until you cancel it. If you would like to pay by Direct Debit, please use the form opposite, entering your BRF account number under 'Reference number'.

You are fully covered by the Direct Debit Guarantee:

The Direct Debit Guarantee

- This Guarantee is offered by all banks and building societies that accept instructions to pay Direct Debits.

- If there are any changes to the amount, date or frequency of your Direct Debit, The Bible Reading Fellowship will notify you 10 working days in advance of your account being debited or as otherwise agreed. If you request The Bible Reading Fellowship to collect a payment, confirmation of the amount and date will be given to you at the time of the request.

- If an error is made in the payment of your Direct Debit, by The Bible Reading Fellowship or your bank or building society, you are entitled to a full and immediate refund of the amount paid from your bank or building society.

- If you receive a refund you are not entitled to, you must pay it back when The Bible Reading Fellowship asks you to.

- You can cancel a Direct Debit at any time by simply contacting your bank or building society. Written confirmation may be required. Please also notify us.

The Bible Reading Fellowship

Instruction to your bank or building society to pay by Direct Debit

Please fill in the whole form using a ballpoint pen and return it to:
BRF, 15 The Chambers, Vineyard, Abingdon OX14 3FE

Service User Number: | 5 | 5 | 8 | 2 | 2 | 9 |

Name and full postal address of your bank or building society

To: The Manager	Bank/Building Society
Address	
	Postcode

Name(s) of account holder(s)

Branch sort code

| | | – | | | – | | |

Bank/Building Society account number

Reference number

Instruction to your Bank/Building Society
Please pay The Bible Reading Fellowship Direct Debits from the account detailed in this instruction, subject to the safeguards assured by the Direct Debit Guarantee. I understand that this instruction may remain with The Bible Reading Fellowship and, if so, details will be passed electronically to my bank/building society.

Signature(s)

Banks and Building Societies may not accept Direct Debit instructions for some types of account.

Enabling all ages to grow in faith

Anna Chaplaincy
Living Faith
Messy Church
Parenting for Faith

The Bible Reading Fellowship (BRF) is a Christian charity that resources individuals and churches. Our vision is to enable people of all ages to grow in faith and understanding of the Bible and to see more people equipped to exercise their gifts in leadership and ministry.

To find out more about our ministries and programmes, visit
brf.org.uk